LAW SCHOOL
FAST TRACK

Other Books

Law School Fast Track

Essential Habits for Law School Success

Derrick Hibbard

The Fine Print Press

Honolulu

Copyright © 2011 by Derrick Hibbard

Published by
The Fine Print Press, Ltd.
Honolulu, Hawaii
Website: www.fineprintpress.com
Email: info@fineprintpress.com

Library of Congress Cataloging-in-Publication Data

Hibbard, Derrick, 1983-
    Law school fast track : essential habits for law school success /
    Derrick Hibbard.
        p. cm.
    Includes index.
    ISBN 978-1-888960-24-2 (alk. paper)
    1. Law—Study and teaching—United States. 2. Law students—United
    States—Handbooks, manuals, etc. I. Title.
KF283.H53 2011
340.071'173—dc2

                                                    2010019365

Cover design and typesetting by Designwoerks, Wichita, Kansas.

The text face is Esprit Book, designed by Jovica Veljoviç and issued by ITC in 1985; supplemented with chapter headings in Castellar, designed by John Peters and issued by Monotype in 1957, section headings in Poppl-Laudatio, designed in 1982 by Friedrich Poppl for the H. Berthold AG Typefoundry of Berlin, and accent uses of American Typewriter, Helvetica Neue, and Law & Order.

PRINTED IN THE UNITED STATES OF AMERICA
20 19 18 17 16 15 14 13 12 11 10   9 8 7 6 5 4 3 2 1

CONTENTS

DEDICATION

This book is dedicated to Amanda, Zoe, and Liam, who put up with law school, and without whose unwavering support this book would never have been possible.

To William Shakespeare, who famously wrote, " … let's kill all the lawyers …."

And to Dick the Butcher, who in *Henry VI* gives that statement its meaning, and our profession the ultimate compliment.

ACKNOWLEDGMENTS

A special thanks to Amanda, who is always there for me.

To Mike Prasad, who was the first to read any part of the manuscript and who offered many excellent suggestions.

To Amelia Holston, Laura Flowers, Mike Prasad, Rachel Barmack, and Zack Stevens, all of whom were part of my 1L study group. It was our discussions that led to many of the ideas in this book.

To Alan Knoll, Allison Young, Jimmy Cook, Lindsey Lazopoulos, Robert Moyle, Tyler Tanner, and Lauren White for your advice, suggestions, and all-around help through the whole process.

To Heath Hatch, Mike McKelleb, and Tim Pettitt, upperclassmen who imparted their wisdom when I was a fledgling law student.

To Sudha Setty, who is not only a terrific law professor, but who provided the sample exam and model exam answers you see in this book.

Finally, to Thane Messinger for his editing, great advice, and intriguing discussions on the topic.

Foreword

As you hold this book in your hands, you might be forgiven for wondering what possible value there could be in this short book—especially as compared to the many larger books written for prelaw and new law students.

When I received the manuscript for this book, I must admit that my initial reaction was the equivalent of a sigh: *another* book for law students?! (I am certainly not blameless, as I too had written just such "another" book—and despite my trepidation that I had only done so when the advice I thought should be out there simply wasn't, I was all too aware that my voice in *Law School: Getting In, Getting Good, Getting the Gold* would join others in a growing chorus of confusion for law students.)

In the not-too-distant past it might have been true that there wasn't sufficient advice for new law students. There were a handful of books, and just about everyone was in the same boat of relative ignorance. Today, the problem is if anything the opposite: there's too much advice, and it all collides in a jumble of contradictory opinion. Worse, it's easy to see "opinion" as mere subjective conjecture; some opinion, however, is better than other. (This is of course a key skill for an attorney.) Happily, Hibbard by-passes this thicket, instead focusing on a clear-headed set of habits that will almost certainly help, piece-by-piece and collectively.

What distinguishes this book is not that it has secret advice that is somehow missed by all those other sources. Rather, Hibbard condenses that advice in a highly useful, useable way. As any law student learns early in the first semester, this is a crucially important set of skills—and a set of skills that not every law student discovers early enough to be helpful on law exams. Some law students flounder not just in their first semester and year, but throughout their law school experience—making their years more of an ordeal than an education. This does not have to be, for the "tricks" are readily known to anyone who has gone before. The real trick is in conveying the points simply and persuasively. This is Derrick

Hibbard's contribution to you, the new or future law student.

His is valuable guidance. Rather than focus on the mountains of advice, his suggestions simplify rather than complicate. If you are entering law school, you would be extremely well-served to heed his suggestions: Good habits are a very large part of law school success.

Why mere habits, and why a focus in the first week of law school?

The question "Why habits?" is a fair one, and is central to where many law students go wrong—and, yes, after many years' thought I am convinced that many law students do "go" wrong—and this is where this happens. Most law students are very, very smart. Most have focused (or relied) on raw intelligence to muscle their way to academic success. Most have achieved that success with no few accolades and, often, with a great degree of personal freedom. In law school, there will be even more freedom—and precious little feedback—and plenty of signs that point to a normal classroom environment. But to anyone who has survived law school (and who has aced law school exams), this is an experience unlike any in college or before. Law exams are neither a form of memorize-and-regurgitate, nor a series of genteel research papers. And the law classroom itself bears little resemblance—beyond the chairs and podium—to the generally good-natured repartee prior to law school. Law classes and law exams are an intense and complex challenge to one's ability to apply knowledge that is largely self-taught. The study of law is thus simultaneously exhausting and disorienting.

As to a focus in the first week of law school, the reality of law school is that the methods of most students lead to a symptom very much like the swamping of a boat. If a vessel is overloaded, even the slightest disturbance sends water perilously near the boat's rim. With rough seas, it is likely to suffer a dual fate: incoming water only adds to the boat's inability to stay afloat. Bilge pumps are designed to remove water, but can operate only with proper maintenance—and only to keep modest amounts of water out. The more the boat tries to move, the more likely the water will hit with greater force—but cutting power is worse, as rough seas will toss the boat around all the more.

It might seem silly to compare one's first year of law school with an overburdened boat in rough seas, but that analogy is quite accurate. Here's why: As one begins law school, the rough seas are immediately apparent. These are the multiple demands of case briefs, legal terminology, the Socratic Method, the forced curve, blind grading, and a group of future colleagues who are, for the first time in their lives, their intellectual equal. The overloading of the boat is where old habits come into play: most law students carry their old, bad habits—but they *seem* like the right habits, the only habits. As the law cases come and go by the dozens and then hundreds, those old habits prove useless, and become downright awful. The "boat" is your own understanding of the law. So, unless you know exactly what each new case means, and how it applies, and how to apply it, that case is another splash of water over your bow. Before long you're drowning in case after case, and, to borrow again from naval terminology, are less and less able to make headway—understanding the law behind the cases—that is essential in your progress.

There are, moreover, differing goals. Some wish simply to move from point A to point B: from matriculation to admission to the bar, by way of graduation from law school. Others seek the equivalent of fame and fortune: membership on the law school's law review, prestigious summer and judicial clerkships, and the fortune of a position with a national law firm. Either goal will carry differing responsibilities, of course. The paradox is that the same set of habits discussed in this book will be equally helpful: if mere transport is your goal, this book will help you achieve that with far less time and stress. If stardom is your goal, this book will help you to achieve *that,* also with (relatively) less time and (relatively) less stress.

I was, finally, skeptical of the author's inclusion of a text exam, as it seemed risky to encourage students to prepare for just one type of exam or exam style. I've come around, however, for two reasons: this has been the most praised part of the manuscript by those students who've seen it, and the sample answer and checklist provide a valuable insight into how law professors think about and grade most exams. This should likewise have a profound impact on how the new law student goes about preparing for and taking those ever-important law exams.

It is nearly always good advice to accept any input—and absorb that input with an eye towards its logical basis and your own circumstance. As might be apparent, in my opinion the suggestions offered in this book are sufficiently important, helpful, and applicable to warrant your full attention, regardless of your ultimate goals. I hope you find them as beneficial to you as I think they are for every new law student.

Thane Messinger, author of

Law School: Getting In, Getting Good,

Getting the Gold

The Young Lawyer's Jungle Book:
A Survival Guide

July 2010

WHY THIS BOOK?

You might be browsing in the bookstore or flipping through pages online, trying to decide which (among so many) is the best law school guide. You will inevitably ask, "Why *this* book?"

Law school is a difficult experience, and there are lots of helpful "guides" out there that will help you to do well in law school. I'll be honest with you—many are good books and contain good advice that will help you as a law student. This book will also help, but in a different way.

I read several of these other guides before I started law school, and while they are helpful, they provided too much information. These guides did explain the law school experience, but I needed quick answers about simple things—questions on such things as writing a brief, or how many notes is too many notes, or how to prepare, day in and day out, for the ever-important final exams. I ended up wasting time reading about things I didn't really need to know—points that didn't really make much difference—or things that were self-explanatory. Eventually I had to cut through the mass of details to find what I really needed. So the point of this brief guide is to cut through that mass of details *for you.* Obviously there are many things to think about in law school—but these are the basic principles that will help you *right now.* This guide assumes you are smart, with years of experience in education. This book thus provides the *essential* habits you will need to do well in law school.

WHY *HABITS?*

Habits help us. Or they hurt us.

Good habits can help in everyday life, in the many day-to-day things we have to do. Being a student is really no different. When you develop good habits that help you accomplish your goals and tasks quickly and well, you will be more successful.

A habit is something you do without needing to think. In law school you will need to think—a lot—but you will need to focus all of your energy on thinking *about the law*. If you develop habits that will naturally help you as a student, you will be able to focus on learning. Success will come.

Advice is useless unless it is incorporated into your routine. Good habits have to be just that—habits—to be any use at all. Thus, developing those good habits is perhaps as important as the substance of the habits themselves.

Although the advice in this book is helpful and will ultimately make your experience as a law student less rough, the road is far from easy. You will still have to put in long hours, and you will have to work hard. The point is that by establishing these good habits you won't have to work *as* hard. And when you do work, it won't seem so much like "work."

WHY *ESSENTIAL* HABITS?

One important aspect of learning is repetition. My take on repetition is to do it without unnecessary fluff. So, as an overview, let's first scan this list to keep these points in mind. Then let's dive right in!

1. Make Your Study as Effective and Efficient as Possible

2. Make a Plan and Stick To It

3. Set Goals and Follow Up With Yourself

4. Read Effectively

5. Brief Every Case, But Be Brief

6. Be Active In Class

7. Study Your Professor

8. Stay Organized

9. Break The Excessive-Note Habit With "Outline" Notes

10. Write Your Own Outlines

11. Use One Day a Week to Review for Each Final

12. Keep Living Life

13. Maintain a Positive Attitude

Consistent with the theme of this book (and with being a good law student), if you're already comfortable with a particular habit, skip to the next one. This is a book written for law students who have a lot to do, not a whole lot of spare time in which to do it, and who just need a little help in learning how to absorb the mountain of material in law school.

WHY FOCUS ON YOUR *FIRST WEEK* OF LAW SCHOOL?

These good habits should be goals you aim to achieve throughout your three years as a law student, but, for our purposes, the focus is immediate: What will you implement *for your first week of law school?*

These habits are designed to make you a better law student, and you cannot afford to get behind, whether during week one or later. Good habits in your first week will put you in better shape for your entire first year—and thus for those all-important first-year grades. Poor habits will not just hurt you early in your first semester, the effects of bad habits will continue to get bigger and bigger, threatening to steamroll right over you. These bad effects not only get bigger as the classes, cases, and volume of law school continues through your first year—they get worse: With bad habits you'll feel helpless against the never-ending onslaught. Thus, let's focus on building the right habits, right up front.

Further, as a law student, your goals should be not only to do well in your classes (*i.e.,* get great grades), but also of course to actually learn the law. In other words, you want to do well in law school, but you also want to prepare yourself for the real world of law practice. If you implement these habits now, in addition to your successes as a law student you will experience even better success in the long run.

The advice in this book comes from personal experience. I want to impart what I learned about being a law student: what worked and what did not. For example, one of the most difficult concepts for me to grasp early in the first semester was the infamous case brief (often called simply a "brief" in law school). As we will discuss, and as you may already know, a case brief is a short summary of a case that helps you remember the facts of the case and the rule of law that applies to that case. During my law school orientation, a professor got up in front of our entering class and gave us a brief description and "how-to" session about writing briefs. To drive his point home, he emphasized that for every case we needed a detailed brief, or we wouldn't understand the law or be prepared for class.

So that is what I did.

For every class, for every case, I wrote out a long, detailed, monotonous brief. It was *horrible*. Hours and hours were spent on those #@%! cases. After a few days and after seeing what each professor actually discussed in class, I realized that each expected something a little different. While some professors delved into the facts and the story of the case to put the rule of law in context— and expected their students to be ready to do the same—other professors only needed a short description and the main point(s) to be learned from the case. Given how much time I was spending on these briefs, it just didn't make sense. The omnipresent "brief" got even more confusing when I spoke to 2Ls and 3Ls (students in their second and third years of law school, respectively) who said they only "book briefed," or highlighted the facts in the case and the rule of law, without writing anything out.

Case briefing seems to be a simple concept, but I was worried that if I didn't do a detailed brief for each case, I would miss something. Or, alternatively, if I wrote out too much detail, I might be missing the forest for the trees. I eventually figured out a method of writing briefs that worked for me—which we will discuss later—but I would have given my left arm to know, then, the best way to do that simple task. I would have enjoyed my first year more, and I would have saved a *whole* lot of wasted time.

In the following chapters, I will point out better ways to study and do well in law school, and how to implement these ways into good habits that you won't have to think about. I am not here to outline everything you should expect from law school, as I am a supporter of experiencing law school rather than reading about experiencing law school. The purpose of this book is to give you the short, sweet, and condensed version of what you need to know to succeed. Again the focus is in the first week, even though the benefits will extend far beyond then. It's short because soon you will be asked to read and analyze mountains of cases. My job is to point out the habits you need to succeed—advice I would have loved before and during my first year. When you are aware of the habits you need to develop, it is easier to take steps in that direction. It isn't an overnight change, but you can start right now at creating your own success in law school.

It's as simple as that.

So please accept this book with its purpose and my background in mind. As of this writing, I am right smack in the middle of my second year of law school, squeezing in a few minutes here and there for writing this. I did well—extremely well, actually—in my first year, but that's as much confirmation of the value of these habits as it is a basis for any personal conceit. As you'll read later in this book, I too faced many challenges. What you'll read is how I learned just how useful these good habits can be—and how beneficial they can be to you too.

So, this is from one law student to another—advice from an upperclassman who has not only been there and done that, but who is right here along with you.

The Most Important Habit

The focus of this book will be to develop one general habit that will not only help you to become a stellar law student, but will also be beneficial throughout your life. This habit will put you a cut above most students and even attorneys in practice—and it seems like such a logical habit to develop. You'd think everyone would be focused on it, but for some reason we, maybe even as a species, love to waste time.

Students spend a *lot* of time doing things they think are important and a lot more time doing things—be honest—they know aren't all that important. Either way, this is simply wasting time. Much of this book is devoted to the number one, most important overarching habit, which happens to include four parts:

1. Identifying things that waste time.
2. Stop doing things that waste time.
3. Identifying things that are both effective in learning and an efficient use of your time.
4. Doing more of those things in #3.

Habit #1: Make Your Study Efficient And Effective

This means you do what you must do to be the best student possible, and nothing more. This means that when you sit down to study, even if for short periods of time, you are getting the most from your time studying. If you can master this one principle and make it habitual, you will be successful.

This habit seems easy. But as trite as it might sound, that doesn't necessarily make it easy.

We live in a time where it is possible to be extremely efficient. Possible. Not probable. We all have gadgets to keep us connected with the world around us, and these gadgets can be used to make learning easier. No longer do we have to sift through hundreds and thousands of books at the law library while doing research, nor are we restricted to taking long-hand notes. This is an incredible time to be an efficient student; efficiency is within our grasp! All it takes is a habit—a way of doing things that is reinforced by practice every day—to actually *be* efficient.

Much of what follows is some variation of exactly this idea: habits you should develop to become more efficient *and* effective. This is the end goal, the most important goal, the habit that will carry you through law school successes and into your career. Effective and efficient study is the goal, the aim, and the most important habit you can develop in law school.

Before You Start

Your palms will be sweaty before you actually start law school. Your heart will start to flutter, and once you check the assigned readings you will gasp and suddenly feel the pressure of a thousand pages to read in just the first few days. And those uncertain finals you keep reading about, and upon which your career apparently depends, loom at the end of the semester.

I remember being in your shoes less than a year ago. I can still taste the uncertain nervousness of the experience. I could tell you to brush those anxieties aside, but it would do no good—you are *going* to be nervous and uncertain. You *should* be nervous—at least a little.

I might even tell you that law school isn't really all that hard, but that would not be telling you the truth, or at least not the whole truth. Law school is, in addition to everything else, intimidating, overwhelming, stress-inducing, ego-reducing, and a whole lot of work. But it ain't rocket science. Thus the importance of building those good habits! Nearly anyone can graduate from law school, if they put their minds to it. But then again, *our* goal is not merely to *graduate*. It is to *excel*.

What I will tell you is that you *can* do it, and you can be *successful*. In order to be successful, however, you need to establish some positive habits from the beginning. (If you find yourself already deep in the law school experience as you read this, just remember it is never too late to develop these important habits, and re-focusing your efforts in a positive way will be worth it.)

The next habit, and one of the most foundational habits you can have, is to make a plan and stick to it.

Habit #2: Make a Plan and Stick To It

A few weeks before I started law school, I read a sample schedule of a sample day for a sample law student. The student's schedule went something like this:

7:00 a.m. to 9:00 a.m.	Wake up and study
9:00 a.m. to noon	Class
Noon to 11:00 p.m.	Study

(I'm exaggerating a little bit, of course, as there was a sprinkling of 30 minutes for dinner here and 20 minutes for laundry there.)

I saw this schedule and thought, "This is crazy! I can't do this schedule, and I can't compete with people who can do this schedule."

Despite this, I spent the first few days of law school trying to follow this plan. Before long, I found that it was impossible. Maybe it was impossible for me. Maybe it was impossible for anyone. But I knew it wouldn't work. I found myself burning out after only a few days. I knew my class notes and cases very, very well, but I no longer cared. Soon, I wasn't paying attention in class, and I teetered on the verge of complete burn-out. I realized what was happening, so I backed off and abandoned this insane study schedule. I then over-compensated for my near-burnout, and began not studying enough. I floundered for a few days until I decided: *I needed a schedule*. A plan, one just for me.

Everyone is different and will prefer studying at different times of the day and in different ways, but schedules are equally important. Law school requires a great deal of thinking, and each day will bring more and more assignments and concepts for you to make sense of. A schedule will help focus more energy on what you are learning and less energy on deciding what to do each day.

Your schedule must be your own. *You* have to live it, so make sure you can.

SLEEP

Sleep is a crucially important aspect of your schedule. You might think you'll zoom past all your classmates with a mere five hours of sleep, but chances are the only zooming that will occur will be that nauseating feeling inside your brain.

Studies show that students who get a good night's sleep perform better than those who don't. Don't believe me? Well, I didn't realize the power of sleep either, until it got so bad that I realized I *had* to make a change. It was in the middle of my first year of law school. I was just like many of you—staying up late for just about any reason and then sleeping in until just before class. Well, you might be able to fake your way through as an insomniac—after all, nearly everyone in law school went through at least some of our undergrad time with a twisted sleep schedule—but the stakes were so much lower then, and the ability to cure an error so much higher. In law school, you have one chance—one!—to ace those exams.

I realized just how awful I felt, and how much more poorly I was doing because I was so sleep-deprived. That, combined with the schedule, convinced me to be more strategic about this basic element of law school life.

Imagine how much better you could do if your brain were functioning correctly. That's right. Your brain simply cannot work as effectively—remember habit number one?—when you don't get enough sleep. Sure, there might be the occasional late-night party. Of course, some might need a bit more than eight hours, while others can get by and be fully alert with fewer. There are also those who are early birds and those who are night owls. We're just learning about these differences, but what researchers do know is that these differences . . . make a difference.

The danger is for two groups: anyone who doesn't pay attention and who thinks they can cheat sleep for an extended period. Sure, you can get by on less than you need—but only for so long. And the older you get, the less able you are to do this for even short periods.

The second group includes those who are "long sleepers"—some might need nine hours a night, or even more, which does cut into study time—and "late sleepers." Many classes and exams are, after all, in the mornings. If you're a long *and* late sleeper, then you're going to need to think even more carefully about your schedule. You'll still have lots of studying to do, and you'll need to be even more efficient, as you'll have comparatively less time in which to do it.

Need more convincing? Researchers[1] assert that a lack of sleep leads to (1) an inability to concentrate; (2) impaired memory; and (3) decreased physical performance. Heightening these issues, persistent sleep deprivation can cause hallucinations and drastic

[1] If you're curious, check the NINDS, or the National Institute of Neurological Disorders and Stroke, in Brain Basics: Understanding Sleep.

mood swings. Without an opportunity to rest and regenerate, our brain gradually loses its ability to function at an optimal level. On the positive side, consistent sleep and rest allows the body and brain to repair itself, grow, and make neural connections, which speed and reinforce learning.

There is, if you're still skeptical, a direct link between sleep and academic performance. Students who perform at higher levels in school with greater academic success share a common habit: They adopt regular sleep habits to allow their brains time to rest and grow. This makes basic sense, and pretty much speaks for itself. Not getting enough sleep affects your ability to perform mental and physical tasks. At some point sleep deprivation becomes a serious issue. Yet law students seem to revel in sleep deprivation!

Getting enough sleep improves your mental and physical abilities. We really don't have to read study after study to know this is true; we live it. When you get enough sleep, your mind is able to perform at its peak. When you don't get enough sleep, it's hard to stay conscious, let alone to undergo (and actually remember) intense study.

Yes, it seems crazy that many students deprive themselves of something so basic when the benefits are so obvious, and as law students, we simply cannot afford to have our brains functioning below their peak level. We *need* our brains!

Why so much on sleep? Here's why: You should consider putting those late night cramming sessions from your undergrad years behind you. Get your sleep! If you develop a pattern of being fully awake during the day, and of sleeping consistently and fully, you will feel better and perform better in law school.

EXERCISE

During the first year of law school I saw my classmates, and myself, slowly pack on more and more weight. As a result of sitting all day long with little or no exercise, the weight seemed to just stick to us. And, as with the section above, the effects of being suddenly overweight were alarming.

Scheduling a block of exercise at least several times a week is almost as important as getting enough sleep. It keeps you from being sedentary, gets your blood moving, and helps you be more alert. Recently a 26-year-old guy from India set a record for playing *Grand Theft Auto IV*— not a video game recommended for aspiring students of the law, perhaps. He played for 40 hours straight, and claimed that he was able to maintain his stamina because he exercised regularly.[2] It might seem strange that being physically fit helps with an activity where you sit down and move your thumbs to control a video game, but it keeps your blood moving and allows you to stay alert. Most of the time, your studying sessions will be similar to playing video games: sitting in one place for extended periods of time and moving your fingers. I wouldn't recommend studying for 40 hours, but you get the point.

Exercising helps your stamina. Law school is an endurance test. You *need* that stamina.

If you have a hard time justifying exercise when you could be studying, try recording your outlines into audio files or listen to CDs done by law publishers while you exercise, or take note cards while you go for a walk. If you still feel like you are cutting too much into your study time, try this: Write down everything you do during the day and the amount of time it takes to accomplish each activity. I guarantee that you will find more than enough time to exercise—and you won't have to cut anything out. Finding time for exercise forces you to be more efficient in your other activities and to make the most out of everything you do.

We do what's important. Exercise is important.

EATING

Make sure you schedule time for three healthy meals every day. This might seem silly, but it's amazingly easy to get side-tracked. You might think that if you read just one more case, or cross-check just one more reference, or grab a bite while reading, or hang out for just a little while longer, it won't make a difference. But it *will* make a difference, in a bad way, if your blood sugar keeps bouncing from binge highs to near-comatose lows. This is no way to study.

[2]Apparently the record was broken in 2010 by more than 15 hours—by a swim coach who cited regular exercise as well. That record wasn't official, but even so, the same principle applies.

I found that if I set aside 20 minutes to eat three times a day, set aside my notes, and then ate a healthy meal or snack, I was able to return to my studies more refreshed than if I tried to "study" while I ate.

Of course, some people are different. Some might need four or even five smaller meals a day. (Those who exercise regularly find this energizing, and a good way to lose weight.) Again, do what is best for you. The point of scheduling times to sleep, exercise, and eat well is to stay healthy. Staying healthy is good for your brain. If you stick to your eating plan, you will be healthier, more alert, and more able to focus and absorb the material when you do study. These will contribute to better overall performance, even if the actual time spent studying is slightly less. This is being both efficient *and* effective—which takes us right back to Habit #1!

Aside from scheduling times during the day to eat, it is important that what you put into your body is good for you. Maintain a *healthy* diet. Sure, lots of students eat lots of junk food, and that's fine on occasion (such as *after* finals). For the rest of the time, however, when you're trying to maintain the energy and stamina to stay intensely focused for extended periods of time, it is better to eat healthy foods that are high in energy but low in "junk." Sugary, oily, and caffeine-packed foods might give you that immediate boost of energy, but the crash comes soon after. And overall you will begin to feel awful. You'll find yourself consuming more and more sugar and caffeine just to maintain that "boost." This adversely affects your heart, health, and brain. You'll feel even more stress—and you'll have less and less stamina to deal with the everyday load of law school stress.

Unfortunately for most of us, as members of the caffeine generation we consume *way* too much caffeine. I'm probably not far off when I say that most students can't get through the day without a few Red Bulls and maybe a latte or three—and I won't lie by saying that I am not among you. The trick is to eat energy-rich food and give up short-term "fake" foods. Remember the guy who set the world record for the longest session of *Grand Theft Auto IV*? He cited not only exercise as essential to his extended performance, but also avoiding caffeine and sugar. He ate *figs* instead. And he was clearly able to push to higher levels of endurance. Now, I'm not a huge fan of figs, but there's still an important lesson. Eating better = performing better. As a law student, you'll rely *very* seriously on performance. Make sure the foods you feed your body and mind are healthy and provide real energy.

STUDY

Set aside blocks of time to study. I learned better when I studied for 30-60 minutes, then I would take a break for 15 minutes. Yes, it's possible to "study" for 11 hours straight, collapse for a few hours of sleep, then do it all over again the next day—but that's probably not an effective long-term strategy. You'll burn out long before final exams. As to a specific, one-size-fits-all, "best" schedule, there probably isn't one. 30 minutes, 60 minutes, 90 minutes? 5-minute breaks, 15 minutes, one hour? Do what works better for you—but set aside times to study and *stick to them,* every day.

Pick a spot to study and return to it *every day*. This area could be in your school's library, in a common (but quiet) study area, or at your desk. Whatever is a good place for you. Many seem to prefer their neighborhood Starbucks or other café, but for reasons mentioned above and for the need not to be distracted, this might not be the best choice in finding a good place to study.

Returning to the same place to study is a good habit because when you sit down in your special study area, your brain automatically starts to get geared for studying. Your brain is an amazing thing, and it remembers and attributes different activities to different places. Everything in your study area will trigger a response in your brain that says, "Okay, now it is time to study." In your study place it is time to start thinking about the law—and that's right, because "this is my study area."

Along with this, you should avoid studying in places where you do other things, which can confuse the parts of your brain devoted to studying. For example, studying in your bed right before sleep is a bad habit because your bed is for *sleep*. (Well, mostly.) When you climb into bed, your mind starts to shut down for the night; you've been setting this habit for 20-plus years. By studying in bed, your brain will start associating your bed with thinking, not sleeping. This leads to a more difficult time getting to sleep, *and* a less-effective time studying, which leads to being more tired during the day and eventually to higher stress levels all around. Your life, as you know it, will end ....

Joking aside, I once heard advice to allow at least an hour between study sessions and going to bed. Before this advice, I was reading my case books in bed right before sleeping, and I was having a difficult time—not only in focusing on the material, but unwinding and falling asleep after I stopped "studying." I took this advice, and solved one major problem with my study habits then and there. Since then, I get more out of studying *and* a better night's sleep.

DOWNTIME

I take my downtime in small segments during my study blocks. Others take their downtime on the weekend, in the evenings, or for extended periods during the day. Be wary, however, as both efficiency and effectiveness can be affected by downtime that is too long. Only plan enough downtime to keep your mind fresh and your life balanced—don't overdo it.

I knew first-year law students who would attend class and then play video games all afternoon. At about 7:00 p.m., they would crack open their books. Needless to say, they were not at the top of the class and are thus not the kind of students we want to emulate, especially when the job market turns bad. Too much downtime will eventually overtake your studies. You are in law school to learn the law—so take only enough of a break during your intense study sessions to keep you refreshed and, well, sane. Law school is about endurance, and you should think of it as a marathon, not a sprint. You *will* have to stick to extended hours of studying, which will come from (and then reinforce) your growing endurance.

Another distraction comes with pre-study rituals. My (bad) habit often consisted of checking email a few times, updating Facebook, re-checking email to make sure no wild news or gossip would escape my immediate attention, reading interesting stories (and some not-so-interesting stories), and searching the web for things I wasn't even particularly interested in. We all get suckered by these little distractions to put off our chores, such as work, study, and taking out the trash—so no one is immune.

You will do better simply to jump into your studies. Save a few minutes, after you've accomplished some real learning, for some mindless distraction later. This is hard—you need to be firm with yourself. If not, you end up wasting a *lot* of time, getting tired and bored before you even crack open your law books—and you won't get much out of it when you do study. This is one area where you can force yourself, fairly simply, to change a bad habit into a good one. When you study ... *study!* Close your email window. Close Facebook. Close everything that's not related to what you're doing at that moment: studying. This is a basic issue of time management, and it's exactly what you'll need once you start studying for the bar exam—and when you start your first job.

These little rituals aren't all bad—in moderation—if they help relax your mind before studying. What tends to happen, though, is that you get used to your mind wandering and want to avoid the intense focus of study. This takes us back to the bad habit that you need to change to a good habit.

If you need a break between classes or study sessions, give yourself a set number of minutes to relax—and then jump in! For example, if you say, "I'm going to take a 10-minute break," then force yourself not to lie: Set a timer! Do whatever you want for 10 minutes, and when your timer chimes, get back to work! As painful as this can sometimes be, you'll end up enjoying your downtime *much* more. You will appreciate each minute because you will have the satisfaction of honest studying, and you won't feel guilty for taking that break.

BE FLEXIBLE, BUT STICK TO THE PLAN

A schedule is important because it allows you to make a plan and then forget about *planning* the plan. If you make up your mind about how you spend each day, then you do not have to worry about how each day will play out.

Things come up, sure. I am in law school with a family, so things come up more often than not—and you just have to adjust. Actually, this proves how valuable a good time-management and planning habit is. The less you have to worry about each day, the more able you are to adjust when something does come up.

Likewise, be honest. If you aren't studying enough, or if you are burning out too early—adjust to keep a nice balance and then stick to the schedule.

HABIT #3: SET GOALS AND FOLLOW UP

Goals are self-explanatory. If you set a goal, then you are in reality competing *with yourself* to accomplish that goal. If you compete honestly, you will be more successful than if you had not set a goal in the first place.

Setting goals will help you save time because you know both the end result and what you have to do to get there. More time is obviously better, because you can focus on actual studying. You can also relax a little more (and with less worry) than if you did not set goals (and thus did not save time).

Setting goals helps you be more productive because you are working towards something, and you *know* what it is you are working towards. This seems obvious, but the common, bad habit of simply "studying" means that many law students don't really know whether they're accomplishing a goal, because they never think of it as a real goal.

Setting goals will decrease your level of stress, especially when you can see progress. This you will see if you set reasonable goals. For example, don't say, "I will complete all six outlines in three days!" Instead try, "I will complete the outline for sections 1-3 of this course in three days. After that, I will move on to my next course."

The first "goal" is just silly; there's no way you can accomplish that unreasonable objective, so you're setting yourself up for failure. You're going to be miserable *and* ineffective. The second goal, on the other hand, is not just reasonable—it means that you're far more likely to actually finish all of your subject outlines, far earlier than you would if you just "did your outlines," *and* you're going to feel better along the way. You're going to see real progress every day!

Above all, by setting goals you will eliminate annoying questions such as, "What should I study today?" or "What should I work on right this moment?" With goals, you know what you need to be doing. Setting goals will help you focus and stay on track. You are a law student committed to being effective and efficient. You will develop habits to become the best law student possible, and you stay on this track by setting goals.

As mentioned, you want to get in the habit of setting short-term, attainable goals. Of course, you should also have longer-term goals: doing well on your exams, getting an amazing clerkship for your second or even first summer, passing the bar exam on the first try, and landing an amazing job. All of these are good, and you should keep all in mind. But these are not your day-to-day goals. Your main focus, especially in your first year of law school, should be on what you do each day of each week.

I made a goal, for example, to review my class notes within a few hours after class and incorporate them into my outline. The goal was something I could follow up with each day, and I could see progress. I retained much more information on the days that I reviewed my notes and added the few important lines to my outlines than on the days I did not.

Reviewing outlines and other short-term goals leads to success in your long-term goals. So keep your long-term goals in the back of your mind while you focus on simple, immediate, achievable goals. Goals are about making progress, so make your goals *possible*. Pick a few goals to start out with, master those, and then add more goals.

The most important part of setting goals is not just the goal itself, but the follow up. If you don't follow up, you're not working toward that goal ... chances are you're doing more dreaming than actual work. At the very least, failing to follow up means that you don't know whether you're reaching your goal—which means that you won't know whether that goal is the right goal, and whether the next goal will ever follow. A goal is about checking your progress and seeing your improvement. In other words, *following up*: What was the goal? Was it met? Was it the right goal? Was your learning both effective and efficient? Will it help you for the final exam? What should be your next goal?

One of the best ways to see your progress is to keep a running record of your goals and confirm how well you are progressing. Set aside a short period each week to follow up on your goals, and to fine-tune your next goals.

Once your goal becomes a habit, set more goals. Make your time as a law student better and more effective. Continue to do this—make a habit of making goals and following up—and you will find more success outside law school too.

AN ADDITIONAL POINT FOR YOUR FIRST WEEK

It might seem obvious, but you want to make sure you arrive in whatever city your law school is in at least a week before school starts. It is helpful to have a place to live lined up before you move into town, but of course that can be difficult. The more you're on the opposite side of the spectrum—arriving just as classes are starting—the more you're hurting yourself. Aside from massive additional stress, you're distracted at just the time you need to focus in your initial study and in setting good habits.

I finished my undergraduate work on a Tuesday, drove across the country arriving on Sunday, and then started law school the very next day. Ugh. Although it all worked out eventually—as if I had a choice—I was *extremely* stressed for the first few weeks of class, burdened with simple things we take for granted. I had to move into the house I was renting, get all the utilities set up, and I even had to spend a couple of hours trying to find the law school. I had to get my car licensed and re-registered within 30 days, I had to change health insurance for my family, find the grocery store, and finish other seemingly menial tasks—all while trying to figure out how to actually be a law student. Had I arrived even a few days earlier, those unnecessary stresses could have been avoided and I would have been *much* more able to focus on law school.

The moral of the story? Be prepared. Get to wherever you are going with enough time to take care of your personal business before school starts. An example of the benefits: some friends moved at the beginning of the summer, found summer work, and were able to figure everything out over the course of several months. If this is possible for you, it might be a good idea. But even if not, a few extra days will be highly beneficial. We don't realize how much needs to be done until you get there, and we often don't plan for enough time. So arrive in advance if you can.

3

READING THE LAW

Reading assignments in your first year—stacks and stacks of cases, articles, and more—will be the first law school beast you'll face.

Nearly every new law student reads that there are assigned readings before law school even starts—yet every year there are students surprised that there are *actually* assigned readings before law school even starts.

There are actually assigned readings before law school even starts.

Your law professors will not spend the first hour with polite small talk, shallow previews of the course, administrative house-keeping and office hours, and then dismiss you for the real class to start on day two, as in your undergraduate years. Your law professors will expect you to have read the case assignments. And they will expect you to be prepared to discuss those cases. With an expert … them.

I was one of these sadly misinformed late-starters. It never occurred to me that we would *really* have reading assignments for the first day of class. I just hoped—assumed, really—that I could pay attention and absorb all that stuff. So I started out a little behind, which felt like being *massively* behind. There were new assignments every day, so in addition to playing catch up I was sup-posed to keep racing ahead. It was awful, and it was a *very* bad habit.

Being behind in your first year of law school is not where you want to be. From your very first day of law school, you will be responsible for mountains of materials—and you need to stay up with it or the mountain will just continue to grow and the hope of ever getting caught up will fade. So the simple, absolutely crucial step is to keep up with your reading. This isn't just some empty tip: it goes to why building good habits is so important. In this type of academic marathon, staying on task and staying current are only going to happen with serious, sustained effort … and good habits to keep that effort up.

As soon as you know your schedule (which your law school will send you in some form well before classes start), check immediately on the assigned readings for each course. Usually these are posted online. Do not wait. Buy the casebooks, and dig in.

But ... staying current with your reading assignments is an overwhelming task that might even be a waste of time. I remember some professors assigning 40 pages of reading a night—and the readings can be *very* tedious. On the other hand, smart reading helps prepare you for class, and you can build a better understanding of the law—which can definitely help in exams. You'll find questions that will be clarified in class, and as you do the reading, many casebooks contain commentary that helps in the opposite direction: Class will make more sense, and you'll better understand the law that you're learning. Reading your assignments each night is one of the best habits you can develop—simply because it helps you stay on top of your studies and realize the amount of material you are expected to learn.

So, knowing that reading is important, and also knowing that there might not be enough hours in the day to read completely everything you are assigned—how do you get the most out of reading?

You read effectively. This is the next habit you should develop.

HABIT #4: READ EFFECTIVELY

One time, at the beginning of my first year, I read an entire assignment—some 35 pages or so. I finished, and realized I had no idea what I'd just read, much less what I was supposed to learn from the assignment.

Another time I spent three hours taking extensive notes on a reading assignment. I did this so I would understand it all—perfectly—and then realized that I didn't have enough waking time to read for my other classes.

This is a dilemma. There's a constant balancing act between doing the reading for your classes and actually understanding what it is you've read. And if you get behind, it's almost game over: The farther behind you get, the harder it will be to get to the present, much less keep up.

The solution is to read effectively, and take notes only on what is most important. Below are concrete steps to get the most out of each reading assignment, to read effectively:

SURVEY EACH CASE *BEFORE* YOU READ IT

Before you even think about reading a case, look in your course syllabus and commercial outlines to find out where the case fits. Before you read a word, you need to know which piece that case is going to add to your legal puzzle. Your classes will follow a logical, linear path—even if sometimes it doesn't seem so. Your challenge is to figure out what that path is.

After you know where the case fits within the context of the course, read the headings in your casebook (and headnotes if you have the case on your screen). For example, if the civil procedure case you are reading is under the heading "Heightened pleading standard," read the heading and frame your thoughts around that subject.

Before reading the section on heightened pleading standards, read background to pleading in, say, your commercial outline to prepare you for this section. This is the habit you will use throughout law school: Each principle builds on the last and provides further foundation for the next.

Once you have read the headings, scan the case and pay attention to sub-headings, bolded or italicized phrases, etc. Pay attention to the "big picture" of the case. Most cases will outline some of the facts and then jump into the opinion, which is typically followed by the holding and rationales. Some cases have the conclusions at the beginning and the steps taken to reach the conclusion following. That doesn't matter. What does matter is that you understand what's going on in the case—the big picture—before you focus on its details. Before reading the case, you should read the summaries, introductions, and conclusions so you know where you are going before you even start. By reading the starting and ending points first, you are organizing your thoughts and preparing your mind for the case.

Finally, scan the questions or notecases at the end. All of this information is there to help you sort, understand, and remember the information. The case won't make sense if you don't under-stand why you're reading it; these tools will help.

CREATE YOUR OWN QUESTIONS

As you are scanning the case and organizing your mind for the reading, try creating a few questions about what you're reading. This will help focus your thoughts about the material, and it will solidify your understanding at the end of your reading.

The better your questions, the better your understanding will be. You may add more questions, and you may change and refine your questions as you read. The point is that when your mind is actively searching for answers, you are better able to understand how the concept is applied. This prepares you for questions in class, and for possible test questions and points.

Here's an example of a question: If a heading says "Heightened pleading standards," you can make up a question such as "How is heightened pleading different from code pleading?" See how that will help with your understanding? Or, "What is the difference between heightened pleading and the definition of pleading in the Federal Rules of Civil Procedure?" The questions needn't be diffi-cult, and in fact the simpler the better. You will begin to come up with questions in your mind without even being conscious of it. But, when you start, make the effort to be conscious about your questions before and as you read. Your mind will automatically focus on finding the answers to the questions you've just posed.

Make up as many questions as you can and write out a quick summary of your answers. Don't use too much time to write out each question (or answer) extensively: All you need are key words.

READING

In addition to posing and answering your own questions and cre-ating *short* briefs (more on that later), there is another habit that can be beneficial: Read each case as you would a mystery novel. After all, the cases are about real people with real problems. It helps, when reading some case late at night, to realize that there really are (or were) real facts and suspense in the case. You should be *excited* to learn the outcome.

Sure, this method does not work when a case is particularly dry—and in those cases you just have to push through—but most cases are *stories*. They can be *interesting* if you allow yourself to be interested.

One seemingly arcane case that many read in first year Property is *Ghen v. Rich*. At first glance it seems like another boring case written more than a hundred years ago. But when you get into the meat of the case, it really *is* interesting. You have exploding harpoons, whalers on the lookout, and townsfolk stealing whale carcasses! Probably the most interesting aspect of the story is that it is true—it is about a bunch of whalers in Massachusetts who were really there, and who wanted—needed—the legal answer to a real-life dispute. Even now, more than a year after I first read that case, I remember its details and the rule of the law. I remember becoming so fascinated with the story that the concepts of law just came along with it, naturally.

When you look at the sometimes bizarre situations behind a case and remember that these involved real people, with real worries and emergencies, it tends to make the whole case much more interesting—and your reading much more effective.

REVIEW YOUR NOTES OUT LOUD AS YOU READ

Our brains benefit from multiple sensory experiences, and when you can hear what you are writing down you have three levels of intake to your brain. You *see* what you are reading and *hear* what you are writing, and the writing itself is an organized output. As you "short brief" cases and answer your personal questions, you are sifting through the material and deriving the most important aspects of each. You write it down and then read it out loud. It becomes easier to remember as you go along, and what you remember you remember *better*.

Once you finish your reading, you should scan your notes and quickly review what you've learned. If you don't remember a particular point in your notes, or if something doesn't make sense, don't move on until it is clear. If you spend several minutes and it still isn't clear, then jot it down as a question to ask your professor.

READ ONLY ONCE

This is a no-brainer. You cannot read assignments and then re-read them and then re-re-read them again. You simply don't have time.

Yes, you might not understand what the case is about—but part of reading effectively is reinforcing to yourself that you will only read the case *once,* so you had better get everything out of it that you need to get out of it. If you stick to that rule, you will find yourself reading more carefully and ultimately getting more out of the reading assignments, more quickly.

GET RID OF DISTRACTIONS

We've already touched on this, but when it comes to reading it is *very* important. To read effectively you must read without distractions. In the law you must read every word and be *actively* trying to understand and apply each sentence. This is not something you "just do": When you study, you *study!*

"Distractions" means anything that will get between you and what you're reading. If you are distracted, it will take you twice as long to read the assignment and you won't get anything from it.

So, get rid of them!

For me, it was the internet and TV. I told myself that I would spend 10 minutes online, or 10 minutes watching a television show after every 50 minutes of reading. If you do that, you'll get more done, faster, leaving you more time to do whatever it was that was distracting you. Get into the habit of really paying attention to what you are reading without distractions and you'll realize that all of the law will begin to make more sense.

READ ONLY WHAT YOU HAVE TO

You will discover pages and pages of notes and commentary following many of your cases. The notes can be pretty interesting, but much of the time the reading isn't really necessary. This means that it's not necessary, which means, usually, that you shouldn't waste your time reading it. You have other classes to worry about!

Your job is to get the rule of law from the case ... and that's about it. If there is a note or something that the professor thinks is important, chances are that will be pointed out during class.

One crucial reality you should realize early in law school is that your exams can only encompass so much information. Even though they are long and cover a huge amount of material, they are still going to cover the most important stuff—or what the professor thinks is the most important.

A classmate of mine would spend hours and hours studying the most microscopic details—and wasted her time. The professor tested basic concepts, and the details that she thought were important simply couldn't be included in the exam. If the professor thinks a particular concept is sufficiently important, they will say so. Really. If you're awake in class, you'll know the major areas to be covered.

An easy way to remember this important idea is encompassed within a clichéd: Don't miss the forest for the trees. Getting too caught up in the details—the trees—and you miss the big picture. So read the cases carefully, skim the notes that come afterward if you must—just don't waste your time. Read what you need to read!

LITTLE DETAILS

Although the extra study of details can sometimes be distracting or seem like a waste of time, law school is a unique environment. We *can* dig into a subject to learn what we want to learn—and if you're *enjoying* those details, chances are you're doing a great job.

Efficient and effective study should not be confused with shutting out those extra details we are interested in. And we should try to be interested, if only because that makes the time pass by much faster and better—and we learn more and better.

Just make sure you spend enough time studying the materials you will be *graded* on, and *then* delve into the extra details to your heart's delight. Who knows? You might find a way to add some of those details into the exam for an extra point or two—but the bulk of the points will come from getting the basics right.

You'll find that the more effective your study is, the more time you will have to focus on whatever else you want.

4

THOSE AWFUL, HORRIBLE, CRAZY CASE BRIEFS

By now you're probably even more antsy about this law school phenomenon called "the brief," and while you might not know exactly what constitutes a brief and what, exactly, they are for, you've seen descriptions that might detail the data to be included in a proper brief. One brief isn't too bad, but dozens of briefs each night? That's a major time vacuum.

Don't fall for this. Know why you're doing everything you do in law school. A brief is a summary of the case to help you understand the rule of law that should be derived from the case. And when I say "summary" of a case, I mean a few sentences: just enough to put the legal concept into context.

This is all a "case brief" is and it is all that it should be. Doing more will not win you any medals in law school—or points in a law exam. Do not waste your time in this way.

In school, you'll hear this "common wisdom" repeated ad nauseam. Everyone will tell you that a brief is an extensive study of the case, for some supposedly crucial importance. Nope. If you were to do these cases like everyone else says you're supposed to (but which few actually do), it would indeed be extensive and will end up being a huge waste of your time. But as students, we are placed in a dilemma: We are asked to read a huge number of cases, and occasionally we are asked to report on these cases in class. Professors will grill a student with what is called the Socratic Method, and if that student doesn't know the case, well, the professor will know as much and will make it even more awkward and difficult for the student. The traditional way to prepare for these public slaughterings, courtesy of your professor, is to write a detailed brief.

I, on the other hand, am telling you that you need only a super-condensed brief. In fact, I'm telling you that you cannot afford to do anything but a super-condensed brief.

Before I get into my method of briefing cases, let me show you the common model for a case brief. I show you the "traditional" case brief only because it is easier to explain the super-condensed brief if you understand what you are condensing. [I will add my comments in brackets to keep it clear that, while I don't recommend the traditional briefing method, it is, well, traditional. So, if you're going to brief cases this way, at least do so with a *few* good habits.]

TRADITIONAL (BAD) CASE BRIEF

Name And Case Citation. The name of the case is found at the top of the case. [Sometimes the name is long, especially when dealing with businesses and corporations or multiple parties—so *if* you brief this way, use an abbreviation. Trust me on this one—by the end of your first semester, you'll have cases rolling around your brain and you don't want to waste valuable memory space with case names. Try to shorten each party name to just one word, like Smith v. Jones. The citation is important because it will help for quick reference in the library or on an online database. Just use one of the citations listed.]

[**Nickname.** Giving cases a nickname can help in keeping them all straight. For example, we read one case involving Tom Clancy's novel, *The Hunt for Red October*. The case dealt with one company breaching their contract by publishing the paperback copy of the book too early (in September rather than October), throwing off the hardcover sales. I nicknamed the case *Red September* (combining the name of Clancy's book with the month that caused the problems); the nickname was certainly easier to remember than the real name of the case: *U.S. Naval Institute v. Charter Communications, Inc.*]

Facts Of The Case. The purpose of this section is to place the rule of law in context. For example, you may want to remember the situation in which a contract is voidable, or when adverse possession takes place. Law school exams, and real-life practice, require you to make these connections between law and facts, and then apply the rule of law to a new set of facts. So you need to know what happened in each case. [It's easy to get caught up with writing out long-winded facts, however, especially in civil procedure cases where five parties are suing and counter-suing, each claiming a different set of facts and all of which are important to the court's holding. The key is to write *only those facts that are crucial to the court's decision*. I had a goal: to keep the facts section under two sentences. You'll be surprised how much you remember after you read a case, brief the case, discuss the case in class, and then add the notes to your outline. All you need is something to trigger that memory.]

Issues And Holding. What are the questions presented in the case, and what did the court rule? [This is tricky as you first get started, because sometimes there seem to be a mass of issues where there are really only a few; cases are usually simpler than you realize at first. The best way to get at the heart of the issues, and keep track of them, is to write each issue as a yes/no question. For example: Q: Did party X breach the contract? A: Yes.]

Procedural History. You should identify which party is the plaintiff and which is the defendant—a fairly basic part of the case. [Other procedural aspects will come along, and you'll soon get the hang of picking up what's important what isn't. As the semester and year go on, you'll find that you have to write this down less and less because you'll be picking it up almost subconsciously from the reading.]

Rule Of Law. This section should be short and bolded. This is really *all you need from the case*. The other stuff is just context that's useful to make the rule of law make sense.

Type Of Case. What type of case is this? In other words, why are you reading this?! Is the case simply to put a subsequent case into context? Is it purely historical? Does it have an important dissent, or was the decision overruled in another case? Find the rule of law, and then figure out how it fits into the case.

> **Main Point.** I implemented this into my briefs about midway through the first year, and it helped dramatically. Sometimes it was a restatement of the rule of law,

sometimes with a little more information—but always it was just what I needed to know about this case. Ask yourself, "Why am I reading this case? How does it fit into the logical flow of what we are studying in the course?"

Most cases will have multiple court findings, which can lead to multiple rules derived from the case. But if your class is studying the sequence A, B, and C, and the case is about issues D, X, and W—usually the logical step is to pull "D" from the case and place it in the sequence. You'll get to the issues "X" and "W" later on. So define the main point of the case. See the tree, then see the whole picture, and then understand how the tree fits into the forest.

All of this is important to know—but here's the problem: To write a good case brief takes a *lot* of time. Perhaps an hour or more. For *each and every* case! Multiply that hour by the dozens of cases each week, for every course, and it's pretty obvious that something has to give. You just can't spend that much time, especially if the real reason most spend this much time is the fear of getting called on in class without becoming the super-experts in that case.

CASES

Here's a sample case that nearly every law student reads early in the first year:

```
Hawkins v. McGee
84 N.H. 114, 146 A. 641
N.H. 1929.
June 04, 1929
```

The operation in question consisted in the removal of a considerable quantity of scar tissue from the palm of the plaintiff's right hand and the grafting of skin taken from the plaintiff's chest in place thereof. [So the plaintiff underwent some surgery. In your notes, you should simply put: "P had surgery."]

The scar tissue was the result of a severe burn caused by contact with an electric wire, which the plaintiff received about nine years before the time of the transactions here involved.

There was evidence to the effect that before the operation was performed the plaintiff and his father went to the defendant's office, and that the defendant, in answer to the question, "How long will the boy be in the hospital?" replied, "Three or four days, not over four; then the boy can go home and it will be just a few days when he will go back to work with a good hand."

[You read the next sentence and you know that these statements made by the doctor are pivotal part to the case. You can underline them so this section will be easy to find later. Notice, however, that anything more than a *little* underlining makes it harder—not easier—to understand.]

Clearly this and other testimony to the same effect would not justify a finding that the doctor contracted to complete the hospital treatment, blah, blah, blah ....

[Several pages deleted.]

As you might tell, this won't really help in ways that you need help for your exam. You read it and you say, "So what? How does this apply to contracts again?"

To complicate matters, as you go on in the semester, even as soon as a few weeks into the year, you will find yourself abbreviating and taking short cuts—but if you're trying to follow the casebooks faithfully, it will be hard to know which shortcuts are smart and which are just short. And you'll suffer a nagging feeling that you're just not getting what you should be getting out of the courses. The casebooks can be deadly, if used in this way.

If used in the right way, before long you won't even realize that you are *absorbing* this information without writing it down. This is how it should be. But if you're still lost and confused by your cases, now is the time to develop a better habit. The way to pick up this information automatically is the next habit we will discuss, the idea of the condensed brief.

But first, to re-inforce why the traditional case brief just isn't worth it, here is a sample from the above case:

TRADITIONAL (BAD) CASE BRIEF: SAMPLE

Below is the actual brief I wrote for this case. [Remember, this is my version of the *bad* example.] Note too that there is more information in my brief than what you get from the excerpt above—because I read the full opinion for class—as you will have to do as well. This is merely for illustrative purposes.

One more time: This is how you will be taught to brief cases, but this is NOT THE WAY YOU SHOULD BRIEF CASES!

```
Hawkins V. McGee
```
New Hampshire Supreme Court, 1929
84 N.H. 114, 146 A.641

Facts:
Burn on hand from electrical wire, w/ 9 years of scar tissue.

Pl. asked, how long in hospital?

Def. responded, 3 or 4 days, a few days before going back to work with a good hand.

Also said that he *guarantees* the hand will be 100% good, or perfect.

Solicited the father of the Pl. to work on the hand many times.

Made a skin graft from the Pl.'s chest onto the hand, and it grew hair on the palm—Pl. suing because of the hair.

Procedural History
Def. said that no reasonable man would take his comments at face value, but Pl. testified to the last 2 facts above.

Def. said that there is always risk in surgery, and that his words were an opinion in strong language—simply making an opinion.

ISSUES:
Was a promise made?

Is this verbal contract binding?

Was the question of the making of the alleged contract properly submitted to the Jury?

(Reason for appeal)

HOLDINGS:

Yes. – though not just one stand alone statement (a collection of statements that were very reassuring) that made that one statement a promise)

Yes.

Yes.

RATIONALE:

Appellate Court did not answer the question as to whether the stand alone statement was a promise, they looked at what the interpretation of the collection of statements.

In context of what the Def. had previously done and said, seeking permission to do the surgery, his words should be taken at face value, and would be a verbal contract.

Any reasonable person would take the statement at face value given the circumstances.

Yes it was properly submitted to the Jury.

DISPOSITION:

Trial courts instructions concerning the proper measure of damages to the jury was erroneous—retrial.

Preparing this case brief took me *hours*.

For *one* case! As you might tell, this is way too much—and it won't really help. This type of brief is a bad habit.

Let's build some good habits, instead.

HABIT #5: BRIEF EVERY CASE, BUT BE BRIEF

You *must* take shortcuts, or you will burn out. The theme of this book is to be an effective, efficient student: a good student, but not one who is headed for burnout.

Once you get the hang of briefing cases, cut down your briefs. Think of this information in perspective of the long run—you will eventually cut all of it down to a sentence or two, and then to a few words for your outline. That's your ultimate goal as it relates to cases in law school.

Towards the end of my first semester, I was briefing cases in a few sentences and then plugging an even further condensed version into my outline. This is hard to do at the onset of school, because there is so much information and you really don't have a bearing on what is important and what isn't. With practice, however, you will find that it gets easier and easier to get to the main point of each case. Below is an example of a case excerpt you would typically see in a casebook. This case is, in fact, the very first case I read in law school. I will give an example of how to brief the case in the most effective way possible, outlining the things you should derive from it for your brief. This exercise is also applicable to the above chapter on reading effectively. Then I'll provide the condensed brief.

The ultimate brief might seem short compared to the case, but it's really all you need. Remember: You will be briefing *hundreds* of cases during your first year. When you finally study for your exams, you will *not* use briefs to study, and you will never be asked to remember a case citation, or other details, on an exam. What you need for the exam is the rule of law, and the context the rule falls within so you can apply it to a new fact pattern: The final exam. Ideally, you'll only put a few lines and the case name into your outline and that's all you'll need.

Now here is an example of what your brief *should* look like. Keep in mind that if you read the case and jot down a few sentences, you will still be able to recall the facts if you are called on in class—and, after all, that's one reason to brief cases at all.

Hawkins (Hairy Hand)

Pl underwent surgery, with a *guarantee* from the doctor that the recovery would be 100%. Pl grew hair on his hand as a result of surgery. Issue: Was the guarantee, and subsequent surgery a contract? Rule: statement (in context) can make a contract.

Now here is what went into my outline concerning the above case, under the heading, "What is a contract?"

1. What is a contract?

    a. R2K § 1—legally enforceable promise

    b. Hawkins (hairy hand): Statement (in context) can make a contract

See how simple that was? ["R2K §1" stands for "Restatement of Contracts, 2d, section 1.]

This entire case can be boiled down to a single rule:

Statement (in context) can make a contract.

That's it! Of course there is more to a contract. But these first three lines of my contracts outline—and this one simple statement!—are what you need to know from that case. Notice that there are other issues in the case, but at the beginning of a course in contracts (and for the exam), this is what you need. When you brief the case, you need only jot a few sentences to help you remember *the rule of law* and *the context*. That's all you need!

THE BOOK BRIEF

A different approach to the traditional brief (and my super-condensed brief) is the book brief. This is tricky at the beginning of law school, because it is easy to focus on the parts of cases that don't really matter. This is true for the traditional case brief, because you will simply pull too much from each case—thus drowning the important stuff—and it's true for the book brief, if what you're taking from the case just isn't important.

In book briefing, you use highlighters in a color-code system to highlight the respective parts of the case. For example, one might use a yellow highlighter for the essential facts of the case, blue for the rule of law, and so on. Many students use elaborate color-coding, and if we were to climb somehow to the ceiling and look down, it would be as if there were rainbows scattered across the room.

This sounds simple, and it sounds appealing to those who've used highlighters in their undergraduate years, but there are disadvantages to book briefing. The first disadvantage is that it's easy to highlight too much—so much so that you might as well have not highlighted in the first place. After all, if two-thirds of the text is highlighted, where's the "important" information? In some ways it's worse than doing nothing at all, because it all becomes a jumble of color, making the text even *more* confusing.

For your facts, for example, students might highlight an entire page! Even a full paragraph is too much. It violates the very point of book briefing, which is to *highlight* the important facts.

So, what happens is that you're forced to scan through the entire section *again,* just to find what it was that you thought was important in the first place.

On the other hand, if you write down a short narrative of the facts, you've already formed a summary in your mind that is triggered by what you wrote. You can look at those short narratives and get what you need to put the rule of law in context. So, you can solve this problem by writing out short phrases or a few short sentences in the margin, or by forcing yourself to highlight *only what is essential*—so that the highlighted phrase is actually separate from and more important than the rest of the text.

Another disadvantage comes from the simple fact that book briefing doesn't really help with what it is supposed to make easy: If you are called on in class to recite the facts of the case and main point to be derived, you have to look through the entire case to get your answers. This is absolutely impossible. You won't be able to focus on a single highlighted line—much less find the right one—especially in a case that spans 12 pages.

When you are sitting in the hot seat during class, there's no time to "look" for answers. It's obvious that you don't know the facts of the case, and it's very, very uncomfortable with 100 pairs of eyes on you.

This same problem—and a third disadvantage—arises when you try to sit down and outline the subject. If you outline every day, you would *still* be going through 50 + pages of text to find the information you need—an obvious waste of time since you've *already gone through the textbook once before.*

What's the rule? Read something only once! More than that and you're not being efficient. But don't *just* read: The act of typing it into an outline, immediately, helps lock it in memory. Highlighting does not help you remember.

As you might tell, I'm not a fan of book briefing—despite the fact that many law students seem to think it's the way to go. In my opinion you can save almost as much time and be more prepared with a super-condensed brief: You will have something to plug into your outline *and* you are more prepared for class.

The purpose behind briefing cases is to know what is going on in class and to understand the context from which the law is derived. Whichever method you decide is best, just make sure you aren't spending too much time on each case—get what you need *and get out*. Be brief. Be efficient. You simply do not have time to devote so much attention to each case.

[Editor's note: We interrupt this broadcast because this point is so important. It has become somehow ingrained that book briefing is the way to short-cut the pointlessly excessive case brief. We agree with the author that both are wrong. The condensed brief, incorporated immediately into the outline, is the way to go.]

5

Your First Week

So you get to class. You'll see many of your future classmates sitting around, mostly towards the back of the room. The tension in the room is so thick you can almost see it. Some of your fellow students might already be reviewing their casebooks while others are typing away at their computers, but most are sitting quietly, nervously, waiting for the professor. Everyone is anxious; no one quite knows what to do.

It's a weird sensation because every single person in that room has been through years of schooling where they have developed skills and habits in many different classrooms—yet the first day of law school is somehow different. Maybe it is because law school is so important, maybe because it is so expensive, or maybe it is just because we are programmed to be nervous on the first day of school.

DON'T BE NERVOUS

You shouldn't be nervous because you're going to know all of these people pretty well before it's all over. After a few weeks, that nervousness will disappear and you'll realize that everyone in the room is just like you and that there was no reason for anxiety. But saying that won't change how you are going to feel, so let the nervousness help keep you alert.

Take a deep breath and, if seating is not assigned at your law school, then *choose* where you're going to sit.

Although the task of finding a place to sit might seem insignificant, it will affect the rest of your time in that class. Many try to stay near the back of the room, hoping that the professor won't notice them.

I've got a secret for you. People who sit in the back, or otherwise try to hide in the classroom, usually get called on more. Pretty much all professors have caught on to this tactic and will seek out those who try to hide. After years of sitting in the back row through my undergraduate career, I made up my mind for law school that I would sit in the front row. I spent the entire first year as the only student sitting in the front row in most of my classes. Call me a dork, brown-noser, whatever … but professors acknowledged me as the only student on the front row, and after that they went after those in the back. Unless I raised my hand, I received hardly any attention at all.

Sitting in the front row was good for me. First, it is hard *not* to pay attention when you are up front. No matter how tired, you are hardly ever tempted to fall asleep with your professor only a few feet away. Second, you are not distracted by others who would be sitting in front of you if you were further back. Third, you would think that with the kind of money we spend to go to law school, everyone would be in rapt attention during class—even when going over the Rule Against Perpetuities. But this is simply not the case. Tying into the second reason, if you sit anywhere in the classroom except the front row, you will see students using their computers for just about everything *but* the law: surfing the Web, messaging, and playing games. Even if you don't want to be distracted, these are real distractions: the guy in front of you checking on scores for March Madness, or—no joke—the girl in front of you buying holiday lingerie. Needless to say, this makes it hard to concentrate.

Sitting in the front row was one of the best decisions I've made in law school. It really did help. That written, you've got to do what's right for you. After all, if *you're* the one checking scores or buying lingerie, there's not a person who won't know it. I ended up being the only one in the front row in many of my classes, and there were times when I was a little lonely. But, more importantly, it helped me stay active and attentive in class, and I reserved time *after* class to chat and be friendly.

Don't forget what this is all about: being active and attentive. This leads us to Habit Number Five.

HABIT #6: BE ACTIVE IN CLASS

Let's get something out of the way. Every single one of your grades during your first-year law courses—which will, to a large extent, determine where you will first practice law—will rely almost entirely on your exams.

Bear with me as I walk through the logic here. First, it is absolutely essential that you understand the importance of law exams. It's also important to realize that you will get very little useful feedback prior to your final grade. So, it's very, very important to think about what you're going to be doing in class and in preparing for those all-important exams at the end of your first year in law school.

To get one more item out of the way, a bad classroom habit we'll discuss later is taking excessive class notes. For now, keep this point in the back of your mind: Taking excessive notes during class is pretty much a waste of time.

To restate the earlier point and to re-re-emphasize it, we'll start with a heading that should be in your mind throughout your first year: Your Grade Comes from your Exams.

YOUR GRADE COMES FROM YOUR EXAMS

Be active in class so that you can follow along and learn what is necessary to do well on the exam, but *do not get confused about where your grade comes from*. Most professors grade primarily on your final exam and *not* on class participation.

It is thus important to remember that your activity in class is a means to an end. The "end" is the final exam. It is not class participation. There are no brownie points for brown-nosing. In other words, stay active in class not for those miniscule participation points, if any, but as a way to gauge your progress and *learn* from your professor; everything you do in class must lead to success on the final exam.

So what does being active in class mean? To be active in class might mean different things for different people. For me it was sitting in the front row and participating in the class discussion. I found that I was most active when I expressed my opinion about certain interpretations of cases, asked questions about things that were bothering me, or made comments. I felt that I got more out of the class and was able to follow the lecture the more that I participated. Participation helps with the overall motivation to be thorough in reading and outlining.

An important point: This type of "being active" should not mean "be a gunner." A gunner is a person who talks excessively in class, who simply wants to spout opinion after opinion, and who is an all-around unpleasant addition. It doesn't take many sessions before everyone knows—and avoids—the gunners. This is a spectrum, of course, so be careful if you are active in talking in class that you not be too active. Remember the rule: Those gunners aren't getting an "A" simply by talking a lot. Talk is cheap in law school; the "A" exam is very, very valuable.

One classmate during my first year took the whole "class participation" thing way too seriously. He made comments about everything to the point where the rest of us were absolutely sick of hearing his voice. Even our professors got noticeably tired of his constant remarks and opinions.

Even though he annoyed us to no end, sometimes he made good comments and had some pretty good insights. I found myself jotting down things he said because they made sense to me. Sometimes those notes helped, but more often they were a source of confusion—primarily because after a few weeks I forgot who said whatever it was that I had written down. I didn't know whether the comment was from the professor or from another student. If it was from the professor, then I needed to remember it; otherwise, it just wasn't important.

LISTEN TO YOUR PROFESSORS

The rule of thumb should be to pay attention to your professor. Listen to the lectures and to responses in discussions, and write down only what the professor says. This is so important I'll say it again: Listen to the lectures and to responses in discussions, and write down *only what the professor says.*

Professors will emphasize what they think is important, so do not be worried about missing a comment from a classmate. One professor would listen to comments and then politely move on with the lecture. She would answer questions, but mainly stuck to her lecture. This was a nice way of saying, "You need to understand what *I* am saying. I don't mind good discussion, but don't mistake that for what *I'm* discussing."

Another way to be active in class is to prepare before each class and to listen *intently* to the discussion—especially to what your professor is saying. This means you are actively listening and trying to comprehend your professor. You are mentally challenging the professor's statements and explanations, and engaging in a silent dialogue. This seems to be a concept almost not worth mentioning—after all, who's going to say they're not going to listen to the professor?—but you'd be surprised at all of those web surfers and lingerie shoppers.

Remember that it is your professor writing the exams, and so it is what your professor thinks is important. Consequently, that's the person you need to pay attention to.

This brings us to the next important habit.

HABIT #7: STUDY YOUR PROFESSOR

Your professor will give you some valuable insight into what he or she is looking for on an exam. In fact, I would argue that studying your professor is the most important part of law school. Of course, you want to stay up on your reading and ultimately you want to learn the law—but your professor's exam is the immediate hurdle, and you pass that by knowing what the professor expects.

Some professors like you to compare the facts of cases with the facts in exam questions. Others simply want analysis of rules and statutes. How the professor conducts class time is usually a good indication of how to do well on the exam. For example, I had a professor who would parse the language of criminal statutes, and simply use the cases as spring boards for discussion about statute interpretation. On the exam, I did extremely well by doing what she did in class: taking apart the statutes—line by line and sometimes even word by word—and analyzing different interpretations. I followed her classroom example and didn't mention a single case.

Other professors will demand that cases be mentioned in the exams, and don't care as much about interpretations of the legal rules themselves. They want to read how the facts of the case are similar, and how to apply the law from the like case.

Each professor is different, of course, and the key is to study your professor. Take note of mannerisms, the way that person approaches legal rules and analysis, and how the law is explained and re-stated.

TALK WITH YOUR PROFESSOR

You're paying a lot of money for a legal education, and legal educators are available to you in office hours in addition to classroom time. So, visit them!

You don't want to make up stuff, of course. That would be very negative. What you can do, however, is to save most of the questions you might have asked in class and ask them instead, one-on-one. This way you not only get in-depth answers, but you also begin to pick up on quirks and mannerisms that are often not displayed in a classroom setting.

Most professors will not give valuable advice exclusively to one student. For instance, professors will inform the entire class if a student asks a particularly good question—but there's still a benefit in having been the particular student asking that particularly good question. When you go to ask the next question, you're likely to get an even more in-depth answer—and you're building a rapport that might be extremely helpful when it comes time to ask for references for, say, internships.

The point is that you can learn both law and "procedure": how your professors approach legal issues in a more intimate setting than the classroom. Importantly, you must prepare *intelligent* questions to discuss. If you're just making stuff up, don't bother. (As in ... don't bother wasting your time going to the professor's office, and don't bother the professor with questions you could answer with just a quick glance at a commercial outline.)

PRACTICE TESTS

One of the best ways to get into your professor's head is to take practice exams. This is something you'll want to do closer to exam time, of course, because you'll miss most of the issues if you attempt a practice question too early. (You can, however, use other professors' exams as a good way to get into practice exams generally, without "spoiling" your professors actual examples.)

Most professors will provide either practice questions or past exams. This is absolutely invaluable. You *must* take advantage of this! This means more than "take a look at it before exams." It means taking the exam under timed conditions, with line-by-line dissection with your team afterwards. In many exams, that's three hours for the exam, plus three more hours for the analysis of how you wrote your exam. At least. And that's for every subject!

TALK TO UPPERCLASSMEN

This can be hard because you won't know anyone, and striking up a conversation with an upperclassman can seem daunting.

It can be easy because upperclassmen are just like you ... they just started last year or the year before! Most are happy to discuss the ins and outs of your new law school, of professors and their quirks ... of just about anything. Don't be shy!

My advice is to put your anxiety aside and put yourself out there: Meet people who have been there and done that. You'll soon find that it isn't as hard or daunting as it might seem, and talking to them is *very* helpful. Among other things their advice will make you less nervous, which will be important in itself. They will usually give you pointers about the exams, and how the exam relates to the class material, and so on.

It won't hurt if you don't talk with someone who has already taken the class, but it will almost always help. I met an upperclassman during my first year and as it turned out, he had had many of the same professors during his first year. He gave me great advice about each professor, but the most helpful information was about a pattern that one professor used on the final exams. The upperclassman showed me that this particular professor would cycle through issues on the exam and he told me which issues would be focused on during the final. I trusted him and focused my studies on that area of the law (while obviously being prepared in other areas as well), and as it turned out, he was exactly right. That extra effort—based on his first-hand knowledge—paid off, big time. It made a huge difference for me, both when I saw the exam and when I got back the grade.

Upperclassmen have taken these same classes, from these same professors. And if the upperclassmen you're talking with was in a different section, chances are they know someone who did have the same professors you now have. Use their experience and insight to give yourself that extra edge toward being a more successful student.

How to find these upperclassmen? The obvious answer is: They're all around!

Seriously, see what organizations your law school has. Choose a handful that are of interest, and stop in. Strike up a conversation, and see what you find out. You don't need to be out to "impress" these upperclassmen. They know what you're going through, and most are glad to point you in the right direction.

Also, don't go overboard. You don't need a statistically valid sampling of three-quarters of the upperclass body. You just need a handful of upperclassmen who've taken the same professors and who might have specific advice that can be *very* helpful to you.

HABIT #8: STAY ORGANIZED

This seems a simple habit to develop, because all you have to do is stay organized, right? In reality, only a few people can do this without serious effort; many others cannot.

I am not one of those who can easily stay organized, especially with stacks of printed pages, books, assignments from multiple classes, handouts, and all that stuff we accumulate in our bags and lockers and desks. If you let this get out of hand, the result is a mountain of junk that takes up too much space, time, and mental energy—and is demoralizing.

I am familiar with those awful moments when you realize you need those few sentences jotted down on that random piece of paper—somewhere in that mountain of junk! You then sift through hundreds of pages to find it, *if* you ever find it. That is being neither efficient nor effective.

The same concept carries over to your computer. If you don't use proper names for your documents, and documents in their proper folders with a logical hierarchy, you can waste enormous amounts of time trying to locate tiny pieces of needed information. Worse, you know that it's there, and you know that every second is completely wasted: With a better system you would have had the answer already. Developing a good habit is a way to combat this issue, though for many—like me—it certainly isn't easy.

I decided that my life as a student needed better organization. I was up to my ears in disorganization, and decided to get organized, cold turkey. It did take a lot of time to set everything in its place, but it was well worth it. The real challenge was in staying organized.

Your goal should be to start out organized, with a clear idea of where you put certain things—both on your computer and in your "stuff." If you are like me and have already fallen into disarray, these principles still apply, but it will take longer to get to that good starting point. Either way, it is worth the effort to stay on top of your organization. Staying organized helps you to be more efficient: If you don't have to look for every tiny thing you need, the extra time you "suddenly" have will make your study that much more effective.

For your home, I suggest getting filing boxes or a filing cabinet. Get a bunch of folders and label them as specifically as possible. I used certain colors for different classes, and then had folders for handouts, returned assignments, notes from class, notes from reading, outlines, practice exams, and miscellany. I also had a separate drawer for all of my papers and files not related to law school, so as not to get them mixed together. (The same frustration and stress ensue when looking for a simple insurance form in the mix of a thousand pages of Constitutional Law notes. Ugh!)

On your computer, you need to do the same things. You have to keep files and documents labeled as specifically as possible, with clearly and logically arranged folders. You should think about and follow a clear and easy naming system for new versions of your work. For example, at first I would just label the document something like: assignment (I), assignment (II), assignment (III), and so on for each consecutive draft. Unfortunately, on the day I was supposed to turn in the document (for the legal research and writing class), I was in a hurry and forgot how many drafts I had. I didn't think to check before sending the assignment. I ended up sending the wrong draft and missing valuable points on the assignment with mistakes I had already corrected. Arghh! This lesson stuck with me, because it was 100% my fault: It would have been remedied had I used a better system of organization.

My recommendation is to have one folder for drafts and a separate folder for the current document you are working on. The folder for the current work should only have one document in it while all others are moved to the drafts folder once they become older drafts. It takes a little more effort, but a little extra effort here and there helps you be more organized. Besides, firms will have strict document-management procedures. There's no time like the present to build a good habit.

If you don't like that idea, then make sure you save drafts in *only* the same folder, and clearly dated to indicate when you worked on it last. Re-save a file whenever you're making revisions, so that it will be immediately clear which is the latest version. In fact, get into the habit of saving your files often. And if there's even the slightest need for a different version, save it with a new, logical name.

Finally, before sending an assignment ... check to make absolutely sure that it's the right one! Double-check your last changes, to confirm that they're where you expect them to be. Just a few minutes here can save a *lot* of headache. [Editor's note: This is exactly what an attorney learns very early to do—sometimes the hard way.]

Whatever your methods of organization, you should be constantly striving to stay as organized as possible. Remember, the whole point of this book is to be more effective and efficient. Being organized is a key factor to both effectiveness and efficiency. No matter where you are in school, or how organized you think you are, try to improve. Implement organization as a good habit and not only will your other good habits play out more easily, but you will also better enjoy your entire law school experience.

6

Preparing for Finals

For most of you—and I was in the same boat—this is the first time in your educational experience where the final exam counts for your *entire* grade. If you're like me, even when we're told this, again and again, it doesn't really sink in.

Yes, I know I wrote that this book is for setting the right habits for your first week of law school. This topic is so important, however, that it is worth discussing, and it does directly relate to how one should start in law school with good habits.

Preparing for those monster finals ought to be your driving concern. It just makes sense: It logically follows that you need to be *extremely* well-prepared for each exam so that your whole year (and your future career) is not flushed down the proverbial drain because of bad study habits.

What follows is going to be hard. Not "hard" hard, but difficult because it will mean that you'll need to break bad old habits, and adopt new, better ones.

The following habits work hand-in-hand with preparing for your finals, and you have to do each simultaneously for this to work. Also, this might sound like a lot of work, but it beats cramming a truckload of information—or, more correctly, *trying* to cram a truckload of information—for a test that has cost you an even bigger truckload of money and time.

HABIT #9: BREAK THE NOTE-TAKING HABIT.
TAKE "OUTLINE" NOTES.

This is going to sound weird, especially because you've gone through (and been successful in) over a decade of schooling to get to law school.

Here goes.

You have to stop taking notes. At least, you have to stop taking the stacks of notes that you're used to taking. There is simply too much for you to learn in law school, and the prospect of taking extensive notes while reading *and* during class is simply absurd. Unfortunately for most law students, it won't seem absurd until just before finals, as you stare at those stacks and stacks of utterly useless notes. Why useless? Because they won't help you study for your number one concern: acing your law exams.

Allow me an illustration: When I finished my first semester of Property Law, I had over 140 pages of notes. One hundred forty pages! In Contract Law, I had *one hundred eighty* pages! I had novel-length accounts for each class, and faced the overwhelming task of whittling that down to a digestible amount of material. What happened? Soon after I started to go over these notes, I realized that they were doing absolutely nothing for me. Many of them I could hardly recognize, and they were certainly not providing any magic clarity to any of the rules we had studied. Quite the opposite. In front of me were nearly a thousand pages of suddenly worthless gibberish.

" ... But you *have* to know all this information!" you say.

" ... But I only took notes on *exactly* what we studied in class!" you claim.

" ... It's just *crazy* to tell us *not* to take notes!!" you protest, with a look of amazement on your face.

Well, let's think about this from a different perspective. Imagine memorizing a novel, or even just reading it several times so you know it well. Let's make it an exciting novel (which your notes will *not* be). Now imagine getting to know five different novels for five different exams—and imagine getting to know each novel well enough to condense that down to 20 pages of excruciatingly detailed analysis for each of them. It just doesn't seem possible, or if it is possible, it doesn't seem quite worth the effort.

When it comes to studying for finals, you do not want to read a novel-length account of Contract Law. More importantly, your law professors do not want to read novel-length regurgitations that simply spill canned law onto the exam—their exam. You need more, and better, knowledge and skill. Much more, and much better.

I wish I had realized my mistake before wasting so much time. The solution is straightforward and follows the theme of this book. Law school is about efficiency—doing only what you have to, and doing it *very* well. To be efficient in taking notes, take only *one sheet of paper* with you to each class! Your goal is simple: *Do not write any more than that single page.*

You can use the same concept when typing notes in your computer, but there you need a bit more self-control. It's harder to know when you've hit one page, and it's easier to just keep typing away. There's no "E" for effort in law school.

One page is all you need from each class—and in many cases, it's too much. Even one page per day equals more than 40 pages per semester, or 240 pages total. Too many notes!

Write down *only* what is essential for your understanding of the legal concept. After all, you have already read the material and constructed a super-condensed brief, and you're working actively in your outlining. This habit will not only save you time and wasted mental energy, but it will also help with the process of outlining itself.

By now, you've probably heard of law school outlines. Let me describe them briefly: A law outline is a hierarchical summary of the law, including not just the many rules but also how each rule, exception, and exception-to-exception fits within the structure of every other rule, exception, and exception-to-exception. The law outline is how the law is structured, for law students and for actual lawyers.

In law school, outlines are a way to learn the law efficiently because a single sentence, or even a few words, will trigger all of the related rules within that part of the outline. An efficient law student will create an outline, read it a few times (and refer to it while working through practice exams)—and then cut the outline in half. That's right! You're going to chop your outline down to size—a manageable size that will actually help you, instead of adding to the fog of confusion. This process of condensing your outline will be repeated until there are only a few words or lines for each concept. This is sometimes called the *summary outline*.

Even then, there's still quite a lot of information to learn. This is why outlines are so important.

One analogy, when it comes to studying for law school, applies: Studying for finals is like a rocket being launched into space. When the rocket uses up its fuel cells, they are detached from the rocket. Likewise, when you study for your finals, you first read your textbook and go to class. Once this is done, it is *done*—and that part of the learning process detaches and falls away. You brief the cases, and put what you need into an outline. Those cases then fall away. You then edit your outline, and every piece deleted is a bit of unusable junk. All this happens until you have created your super-efficient outline. You don't need the other stuff—you don't *want* all that other stuff—because you *know it*. At this point, your super-efficient outline is to help remind you of the law you already know.

So you're going to whittle down your notes into an outline. Why not take "notes" that will go directly into your outline? This means that you read your assignments effectively—so you know what is going on in class—and you actively participate in class. You put your efforts into selective notes, which go immediately into your outline—which you then progressively edit to a super-efficient outline.

For the record, I never did read all those hundreds of pages of notes. They went right into the trash. The point of this is to help you focus *your* efforts in building good habits. There are important ways to study and spend your energies in law school and in learning the law well enough to do very, very well in your exams.

Habit #10: Write Your Own Outlines

Writing outlines isn't particularly hard. But it is time-consuming. It can also seem overwhelming, especially if you wait until the last minute to start. And commercial outlines lurk in the shadows, tempting you to throw down your own notes and read a pre-packaged outline in place of writing your own. As tempting as these pre-packaged outlines are, these are no substitute for your own work, both in creating and in refining your outline; without that effort, you simply won't get enough out of it.

This is not just a "survival" guide. It is a "kick ass" guide! The whole point of *all* of these habits is not so that you'll feel good, or save time, or get a brownie point. It's so that you'll *ace* your exams!

Almost anyone can *survive* law school: Step 1, sign up only for classes for which commercial outlines are available; Step 2, procure said commercial outlines, while not purchasing casebooks (unless you need paperweights); Step 3, spend resulting savings on beer and pizza; Step 4, skip class as much as you can get away with; Step 5, cram from your commercial outlines; and Step 6, obtain passing grades. That's it. Oh, and the last step, applicable to everyone but children of senior partners and sitting justices, is Step 7, starve.

It takes something special to do extremely well in law exams. And much of that "something special" is good habits, not just legal brilliance. Part of doing extremely well on exams is in knowing the material as well as you know your own name—and part of knowing the material that well is in writing it out, yourself.

Note: This doesn't mean that you don't use commercial outlines at all. Not true: They are very handy. If used in the right way—to supplement your work—they are invaluable. But you're not abdicating your responsibility to the commercial outline. Understanding the law is your responsibility, and, as we'll see, there's really no substitute for doing it yourself.

So, with that in mind, how do you write an outline? The first and most accurate step is to write down the major chapter headings first. You will find these headings in your book, and also in commercial outlines. You will include specific points—initially and during the semesters—to tie the "official" law to your professors' individual takes on each subject.

STANDARD OUTLINE

For example, in a Torts outline, starting with Intentional Torts, you would start with these headings:

1. Intentional Acts

   a. Battery

b.   Assault

    c.   False Imprisonment

Once you have written down the headings, add the definitions, like so:

1. Intentional Acts

    a.   Battery: An intentional touching that is harmful or offensive

    b.   Assault: An intentional threat or attempt, coupled with apparent ability, to do bodily harm to another, resulting in immediate apprehension of bodily harm

    c.   False Imprisonment

       i.   Def: Confinement by:

          1. Actual or physical barriers

             a.   Except when there is a reasonable escape route, or reasonably discoverable escape route

          2. Overpowering physical force

             a.   Submission to physical force

             b.   Submission to a threat to apply physical force if the confined person tries to escape

             c.   Submission to duress other than threats (like harm on a family member, or damage to valuable property)

          3. Taking a person into custody under an asserted legal authority

While we're on this, here's an example of how this might be condensed. The logical stopping-place is the point at which the outline is too cryptic to make sense. But don't worry about that to start, because you will begin to understand the subject intuitively—at which point you're well on your way to mastering that subject, and you won't need all those words.

Here's a sample of a first-round condensed section, after you've studied Intentional Acts for a while:

1.   Intentional Acts

   a.   Battery: Harmful or offensive touching.

   b.   Assault: Threat or attempt (w/apparent ability) to do bodily harm &
      immed. apprehension of bod. harm

   c.   False Imprisonment:

      i.   Actual/phys barriers (exc reas. or reas. discoverable escape route)

      ii. Overpowering force, with

         1.   Submission

         2.   Threat if try escape

         3.   Duress (v. fam or valuable prop)

         4.   Custody under asserted legal auth.

Next you will add the finer details and exceptions to the rules.
Most often, you will get these exceptions by reading the commercial outlines and, yes, cases. Your finished outline for these elements of an intentional tort might look something like this:

1.   Intentional Acts

   a.   Battery: Harmful or offensive touching.

      i.   *Ghassemieh v. Schafer*—Chair from under teacher

         1.   Do not have to *intend* to harm—only intend (or set in
            motion) a touching.

         2.   e.g, didn't actually touch the teacher, just set in motion a
            harmful touching w/floor.

         3.   Battery & negligence not mutually exclusive.

      ii. *Garratt v. Dailey*—5-year-old Battery

         1.   Knowledge with substantial certainty that a touching will
            occur.

         2.   e.g., if you pull someone's chair out from under them, they
            will fall.

iii.   Sometimes, young children *(Horton v. Reaves)* and adults with mental disease *(White v. Muniz)* not liable for intent.

    iv.   *Fisher v. Carrousel Motor Hotel, Inc.*

        1.   Battery is anything touching the victim—or closely identified with the body, like a plate or a book *(Kress & Co. v. Brashier)*.

        2.   Harmful or offensive to a person's physical and mental dignity—objective standard

    v.   Battery objective: "Don't mess with me!"

You would, of course, complete each section as you prepare for the class in which that topic will be discussed. It's important that you prepare *before* you actually go to class. Don't rely on the class to tell you what's important: You should go into class *knowing* what is important!

Also, you will continue the process of refining and editing your outlines down to a super-condensed and highly useable version.

BULLETED OUTLINE

The above Torts example is a simple outline, and it works well to prepare for most exams. You can benefit from different styles of outlines for different classes, however.

Civil Procedure, for example, is essentially about a set of rules. For me, it was beneficial to put together a simple bulleted outline with the rule at top and then the basic ideas within the rule in a few bullet points following the rule. Below is an excerpt from my Civil Procedure outline in bulleted format:

Rule 8—Pleadings

Claim for relief must be short and plain statement as to:

- Jurisdiction

- Showing entitlement to relief

- Relief sought

- Defenses

Must be specific about what is admitted and denied

- Affirmative defenses

- Alternative statements, inconsistency

- Can have both in a pleading, but must be concise and direct

Another idea I employed for a few classes was a chart that outlined cases and rules. I didn't use this method for entire classes—but you certainly could, if you had a big enough piece of paper. But below is an example of how a chart might be used as a visual outline. With new software, making charts and maps like these is relatively simple and works well for those who like to learn more visually.

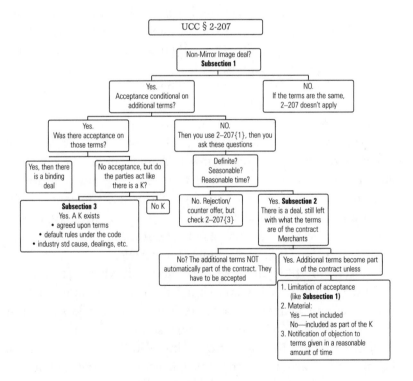

Charts and maps don't work for every type of outline just as bulleted outlines or traditional outlines don't work every time either. For many of your courses, you could have an expansive chart that goes on for page after page and branches off to different topics, so much that at some point you lose the advantage of compiling your notes into an outline. The same goes for the bulleted outline, which is good for things like rules and statutes (which tend to have same-level tests), but not as good for concepts that contain detailed elements (which tend to be more hierarchical and thus need different outline levels to show the interrelationships).

Remember: The outline is a tool to study more effectively, yet can become something that *hinders* your study and exam preparation if you aren't careful. You have to know the material you're putting into an outline and carefully choose what kind of outline suits the material best. Many times, like the example above, you will use one type of outline—like the chart—for a small part of the information while the rest of the information is contained in a more traditional form.

Outlining is a process. As you learn this information you will, after a while, not need all of it. So, the closer you get to your finals, the smaller your outline should get. By exam time you should have six super-condensed outlines, with the details all but memorized because you've used them so much. The resulting outlines are not only easier to study, but the process of getting to super-condensed outlines helps you learn the material inside and out.

If you want to learn this stuff in the best way possible, write your own outlines. You will know and understand the concepts better if you write your own, and you will *not* know and understand the concepts as well if you "borrow" someone else's. Outlines force you to understand what you're writing, especially when you get to the condensing part of outlining.

That written: Use supplementary materials.

I mistakenly thought these were the Devil when I started law school. I thought that I would be a sell-out law student if I even opened a commercial outline or notes from an upperclassman. But the truth is that we have an invaluable source before us. We have the ability to learn this on our own, but also to make sure we are outlining and learning the concepts correctly. Reading commercial outlines is also a good way to prepare for class because you will get an idea of where the class is going, and the professor's lectures will make more sense. If your professor covered topics A and B last week, it is likely that you will go over topic C and possibly topic D this week. So prepare for topic C at the very least! What's the worst that can happen? You prepare for C and your professor pulls out topic E. Big deal. You wouldn't have been prepared for topic E anyway, and this way you'll already have topic C under your belt, and you'll probably understand topic E better because you've nailed topics A, B, and C.

Sure, use and learn from the commercial outlines and other materials, and rely on them without feeling guilty—because they're both effective and efficient!—but don't use them *instead of* doing it yourself. Supplements should be, well, supplemental.

During my second semester of law school, I used these outlines and canned briefs. They were indeed helpful. I did not, however, know those cases nearly as well as I knew the cases that I read and outlined on my own during first year. In second year, this matters far less than it does in first year. I also did not understand the concepts as well as I did when I had to think it out on my own and write it down in the form of an outline (in whatever format).

And this I guarantee: You will see a fellow student in one of your classes who has read only a canned brief, and that student will be called on in class. Professors will know if you read a canned brief or the actual case, and most will exploit this by endless (and more pointed) questioning. Mark my words. It will happen and it will be an important and unpleasant lesson—for the poor canned student and for everyone else too.

These outlines, briefs, and notes are good supplements for your studies, but they are not nor should they be substitutes for your own hard work.

A good habit is using these supplements to supplement your work, and make it make more sense. A bad habit is simply using supplements to avoid doing real work.

HABIT #11: ADD TO YOUR OUTLINES DAILY

One of the most effective study habits a student can develop is to outline *each day* after class and implement the few class notes *each day* into the outline. If you do this, the task of writing outlines will not be so overwhelming. In fact, it's quite manageable: You are just adding a few notes to your outline each day. Take the case we briefed a few sections back. Once you read the case and go to class, adding a few lines from the professor's lecture and your readings (and commercial outlines, etc.), you simply plug in a concise version into your outline. You do this *every day*. Not only are you engraving those concepts in your mind, but you're also are preparing a nice review for your final exam (and bar exam too).

OUTLINING FOR OPEN-BOOK EXAMS

Your outlines should be pretty much the same for both open-book and closed-book exams, and you should be equally prepared for both. Do not fall into the trap of relying on any materials you can take into the exam. These are not a security blanket—they are a trap. If you do rely on these, you will most likely not study as hard as you need to and will end up wasting your precious exam time searching for the answers in your outline. Ideally, you should know the material so well that you shouldn't even have to *look* at an outline during an exam, open or closed book.

One benefit to an open-book exam is that you can bring in super-super-condensed outlines, each containing the concepts for just one issue. I wrote them out in short statements so that, however I answered each question, I immediately knew what elements I needed to discuss.

Again, although it is fine to take your outline into an open-book exam, you should not *rely* on being able to look up information. If you take in a list like this, you have the benefit of being reminded about the elements of the issue. This list is a cue for answers you already know!

If you have a list like this and you understand and can write out every single element, then you have accomplished your goal of being efficient *and* effective. When you reach this point, you are ready to take your exam, whether it is open book or not. This is the end goal, to be able to a word like "consideration" and just *know* everything you need to know about consideration and how it fits into the concept, formation, and details of a contract. That's when you're ready!

Another preparation for an open book exam is knowing where in your outline you have certain concepts. I did this by putting tabs into my outline and compiling a short table of contents. That way, if I did have to open my outline, then I would know exactly where the section I needed was with minimal effort.

If you develop the good habits outlined in this book and truly prepare for each final, you won't worry about "open versus closed" book exams, and you won't need to take your outline into the test with you. You will in fact be at an advantage either way.

HABIT #12: PLAN ONE DAY PER WEEK TO REVIEW FOR EACH FINAL

I remember a feeling of panic at the onset of law school and in the first few months. I was keeping up with my class work—barely—but I didn't have enough time to start preparing for finals. And I didn't even really know where to even start in preparing for finals. The experience was overwhelming until I got some advice from a third-year student who suggested something simple: Set aside *one day a week to review for the final.*

The best way to do this is to review your outlines for each class at least once a week. Just reading over your outlines once a week will better prepare you for the final exam. Add practice exams and you're going to be very well prepared. Keep in mind that reading your notes over and over again will be absolutely boring—so boring that you will find something less awful to do. Outlines are not boring, because they're the entire law, set out in the way you (and the professors and courts) see it.

Sure, sometimes you've got to shake it up a bit and try something new—something that will help you review your outlines but doesn't add to any boredom factor. I made flash cards out of my outlines, and sometimes recorded my outlines into a podcast and listened to my notes. I know someone who drew a simple comic book that illustrated the legal concepts! Perhaps if you're musically inclined you can write a song about each legal test. There are many ways to review, and it really comes down to what you want to do and what works best. The idea is simply to do an overall review of each subject at least once a week and be working constantly toward the end goal of success on the exams.

Of course, you'll add more exam-preparation time and less out-line-review time to this schedule once you get closer to exams, but doing an overall review of each subject once a week helps you keep things fresh in your mind.

7

KEEP LIVING LIFE

I saw a comic strip before starting law school. It showed a man reading a note on the fridge, presumably left there by his wife. The note read, "Cold cuts and leftovers in the fridge. I've gone to law school. See you in 3 years."

A popular saying is that law school is a jealous mistress. And this is true. Law school demands very much of our time and it *is* hard. And there's worse news: It doesn't get any easier. For the rest of your life, you will be busy. Law school is a sneak peek to the strenuous nature of life for any lawyer. If you've not had the opportunity to clerk at a firm to see this first-hand, read any of the *Jagged Rocks of Wisdom* books or *The Young Lawyer's Jungle Book*—they will give you a real heads-up look at life after law school. So don't get too worked up about how scary law school is or how busy in law school you'll be. This is life.

But for many, as for me, this is the first time that the axe meets the grinding stone. It was the first time that I had to devote so much of my time to *anything* ... and it was such a shock that it reminded me of jumping into a freezing cold lake during winter. Or maybe like walking—slowly—over hot coals. To top it off, when I started law school I was married and had two kids.

There's yet another saying, that to be a successful lawyer you have to go through a couple of wives and maybe even a couple of kids. I was not interested in losing those relationships, so in addition to the time I devoted to school I *had* to devote time to my family. I won't lie. This *was* difficult. And it was and still is common for people to wonder how I do it. When so much of your time is taken up for law school, how is it possible to maintain *any* relationship, much less three? This leads us to our next and crucially important principle and habit.

HABIT #13: DON'T WORRY (TOO MUCH). BE HAPPY.

Law school is an important three years. Looked at differently, how-ever, it is *only* three years of an entire lifetime. Don't burn relation-ships or sacrifice the people who make you genuinely happy for the chance of being successful (and, presumably, happy) later. Don't willingly give up true happiness now.

The good news is that you don't have to. You *can* keep living your life, and you *should*. It makes for a better-rounded person, it rounds out your résumé, it helps in interviews, and it will help in your three years of law school. One example: When interviewing for a prestigious internship, much of what the interviewers and I talked about was—you guessed it—my family. Those interviewing me were interested in more than grades: They apparently thought it was important to be balanced too. This point is made in a book, *The Insider's Guide to Getting a Big Firm Job* (which I didn't see until after my interview), spelling out just how different interview-ers' perceptions are from law students' generally mistaken beliefs.

This is a good time to practice living a balanced life, because, as mentioned, it doesn't get easier. You must learn how to deal with an overloaded plate and still be successful *and* happy. Efficiency is a large part of the answer. Yes, I've mentioned it many times throughout the book, and I don't want to beat a dead horse, but ... being efficient in your studies will allow you to enjoy your life *and* do a better job as a law student. Do the things that make you happy, maintain relationships, and just keep living life. Don't become so consumed with law school that you forget who you are.

MANAGE YOUR STRESS

Stress can be horrible and debilitating, depending on how you let it affect you. I knew a student who eventually did well in law school, but only after a *very* difficult start. In his first year he began to suffer from severe anxiety attacks. He confided in me, and told me that he would listen to concept after concept in class, and when it didn't make sense (which for any student is often), he would lose focus and then panic. It sounds too extreme a reaction, I know, but it is real. He became so nervous that any mental stimulus was sim-ply too much for his mind—and a law school classroom has mental stimuli overload. He ended up seeing a counselor and a physician, and began taking medication for his anxiety. Now for the scary part: This is a guy who had never had this problem *in his life!* He gets to law school and starts to breaks down.

Yes, law school is stressful, and yes, many law students seek help—and *should* seek help. (Law students are among the top "customers" for campus mental-health centers.) Even so, there are serious reasons to manage stress, not least of which is the need to continue studying amidst all the personal and law school turmoil, and the possibility of counseling affecting one's bar application—which of course will only add to your stress! As much as you can, learn to manage your stress, rather than being pushed around by it.

Here's another story—maybe a myth—that illustrates the stresses and strains of law school. A student once asked the dean why there were an extra few days off during the fall semester. The dean answered that when they added those breaks, the suicide and depression rates decreased. Even if it is a law school myth, it's a myth with a message: Don't let law school get to you.

Not everyone will experience stress at this level, of course, but the stress certainly does exist and you do need to learn how to deal with it. Stress may come from the overload of course work, the inability to understand all of the legal principles, a lack of sleep, or those looming finals. These are all sources of stress, and you shouldn't feel bad about it—but you *do* need to take care of yourself, because stress will inhibit your ability to perform to the best of your capabilities.

First, try to pinpoint the object of your stress. Then, fix it ... or adjust to it. If nothing comes to mind ... then sit down and identify all the areas in your life that add to your workload. Anything and everything, from cases to laundry. The act of sitting down and writing out these sources is therapeutic in itself: You are *doing something* about it! You realize there is a problem and you are identifying the source. Many times, the act of locating the source of stress is enough to avoid or at least moderate future problems. Of course, once identified it is a good idea to try and resolve or at least reduce the problem. For example, if you are having trouble understanding legal concepts, then visit your professor regularly, with specific questions, to clarify the points. Once you have those specific questions, read the suggested supplemental material on those points to clarify further.

If you find, as a second example, that you don't have enough time during the day to accomplish what you need to do, then it's time to re-evaluate your schedule. You must prioritize, and make time for what is important. Simply identifying these issues and the specifics of your situation will, in many cases, be part of the solution. Many times we try to mask our stress without trying to resolve the problem—and typically these sources of stress are avoidable. Also, this is exactly what an attorney does: Identify problems, locate their source, and offer solutions.

Even if the above suggestions solve the problem, you should still read about stress and stress-relief techniques. Some are likely to work well for you, both for law school and afterwards. Stress comes from many directions, often without warning, and without a single standard of the "right" level of stress tolerance. It is a good idea to reduce your stress, to increase your stress tolerance, and to have a plan for when stress does hit.

Here's how I handle it: When I am at school or in the middle of a project, I deal with stress by taking a power nap. If I'm in class, I focus on stretching the muscles in my feet, wiggling them around, and then looking forward to a power nap after the lecture. If at home, I take a bath or go for a short run. These techniques may seem silly, but they work and I don't have nearly as much stress as I would if I didn't have any sort of relief. More importantly, I don't *feel* stressed. Consequently, I go into the classroom or an exam with energy, not panic.

Do your research about relieving stress. A few quick searches on "stress relief tips" will pull up loads of advice on the web. Once you find something that works, go for it and use it when stress inevitably strikes.

DON'T OVERBURDEN YOURSELF

Part of living life and maintaining a balanced pacing through law school is in not creating *additional* burdens. This is pretty much common sense, so I won't say more than a few words—but sometimes a few words is just the right amount to help.

The start of law school is not the time to make life changes. We should be in a state of progression as individuals, true, constantly trying to better ourselves. But law school itself counts as a big progression, and it accounts for a lot of time and energy. Clear this hurdle and *then* move on to another. Don't sacrifice your performance in law school by trying to do too much at once.

In November of my first semester, I got it into my head to lose 20 pounds. I started exercising more than usual, and I started dieting. You can probably guess the result. Sure, this might be a great idea at any other time, and my wife was excited about the prospect of a slimmer husband. But in the end it was simply too much. All of my thoughts became focused on the goal of losing those 20 pounds, not to be the best law student I could be. Instead of centering my thoughts on a particular issue of law or on preparing for finals, I was focusing all of my energy on not consuming a candy bar. In the end, I'm pretty sure I ended up gaining weight during my first-year weight-loss stint. After realizing where my energies should be spent, I continued to exercise, though for lesser amounts of time, and re-focused on being an excellent law student.

Law school is just not the time for these life changes. Don't load too much on your plate—don't load *anything* extra on your plate that you don't have to—because it is already full. Focus on what you have right now and be the best you can be.

HABIT #14: MAINTAIN A POSITIVE ATTITUDE

Law school is hard, but it is also a fantastic opportunity: You get to spend three years to think! How great is that?! It is important to have fun with the process of learning and in developing as a person as well as a law student and as a lawyer.

Law school is a unique experience. It may well be the only time in your career that you study a specific yet expansive topic: The Law. It is a time where you can explore ideas, ask questions, and learn both philosophical and highly specific nuances. Many law students don't take full advantage of this—I certainly didn't during my first year. I was so caught up in getting good grades and doing homework that I forgot to *enjoy* law school.

Law school is a time to learn the law and enjoy the process of learning the law.

AN ATTITUDE OF SUCCESS

This is an extension of having a positive attitude. The same principle applies. You need to be positive about yourself as a student as well as about your overall experience. If you see yourself as successful and fully capable of performing well on your exams (and if you follow through on this), you *will* be.

There is an idea that a person is the physical depiction of his thoughts. You are what you think—and if you're thinking about being successful and having a fulfilling and worthwhile experience in law school, then you will. Alternatively, if you are focused on the negative aspects of yourself as well as the many challenges of the law school experience, you will likely not have an enjoyable time, nor will you perform as well as you could. Much of our performance is based on whether we *believe*.

Do you remember the children's story about the little train engine trying to reach the top of the mountain? Think like that little train, constantly telling yourself that you *know* you can do it. This is a major factor of success: knowing that you are capable of success and then bringing that positive attitude—with all the good habits that that brings—into reality.

UNREALISTIC EXPECTATIONS

While you *are* aiming for an attitude of being a successful law student, you should not have unrealistic expectations about what "being a successful law student" really means.

A successful law student is doing the very best you can do. For most of us, this is a lot! It is certainly much more than most law students *actually* achieve, which is sad. If you develop and apply the good habits outlined in this book, you will do the very best you can do. It might not be the #1 spot in your class, and it might not even be in the top 10% of your class (although that is likely), but you will be successful if you did your best. After all, there is only one #1 in your class, and the competition is intense to get there. Don't beat yourself up if you didn't do as well as you hoped, as long as you truly did your best. Your goal is to look back on your law school experience, each year, each semester, each course, and know that you did your best, and that you got the most out of it—both in terms of actual learning and in terms of friendships, greater awareness, and fun.

If, by chance, you *haven't* done your best, then now is the time to change. Now! Dig in your heels a bit harder and put forth real effort. Your *very* best. You will be surprised at how much you can accomplish—and how minor all those challenges now look.

I remember looking back on my first year—feeling a sense of accomplishment but also feeling that I could have done better. Upon thinking about it, I realized that I really had given it my best effort, and had performed at the peak of my capability. With that I was happier and more satisfied, and realized later still that I'd become a better law student and had drawn even more from that, both practically and in terms of really learning the law. That's all you need. Do your very best and you *will* do well in law school.

YOUR CLASSMATES

When aiming for that positive attitude, some of the worst hurdles to overcome are your classmates. These are the people you will see every day, the people who will become your friends and colleagues, and ultimately the people you are competing against. It becomes difficult to maintain the positive attitude when others around you are complaining about how much work there is to do, how hard it is, blah, blah, blah. I don't think they're trying to psych you out with this kind of talk—well, most of them—but it kills a successful attitude. When others complain about how hard it is, it's easy to join in the sorrow and wallow in self-pity. When you do this, it becomes more difficult to be motivated and to give your best effort (your "very best!") every day.

The solution is to rise above conversations like this, and *do not participate*. You might think that everyone else is watching you or listening to what you have to say, or even hoping for agreement.

Odds are, they're not paying that much attention; they're just miserable. As unfortunate as that is, you cannot let this infect your own good attitude and habits. If it persists, you must decline to be a part of that group. Be friendly, of course, but don't join in the negativity.

Another attitude and motivation killer is when your classmates discuss how *easy* law school is! When you hear this, you're probably thinking, "What?! This is one of the hardest things I've *ever* done *in my life!* If it's easy for *them,* what's wrong with *me?*"

If you hear this, chances are good that games *are* being played. What to do? Do not join in conversations like this. It's simply a no-win situation: You agree, you disagree, it doesn't matter. It's a pointless statement with nothing good as a result. Avoid talking about law school this and law school that. Know that everyone is working hard to keep up and everyone—really, everyone!—is nervous about the exams. There is so much material, and much of it is not intuitive, and everyone is working hard to grasp the concepts and understand and be prepared for the unknown. You are not alone.

Moreover, what you find easy or self-explanatory will be hard or downright obtuse for someone else. Likewise, topics others seem to pick up by osmosis you struggle with. It can be *hard*. You should not judge your own status or performance on conversations, nor should you even *listen* to them. They are distractions, and harmful distractions at that. You don't need any more distractions; so just don't talk about it. Know that you are doing your very best—and actually do your very best—and just worry about yourself.

I had one friend in law school who would *never* talk about the exams. Not even two words. When we were all finishing up with our exams and meeting outside the examination rooms and discussing the ups and downs of that particular exam, she would politely walk on by and completely avoid our conversations. I had other friends who would hound her about her thoughts on the exam, but she would simply (but politely) refuse. At first I thought that she was probably self-conscious about her performance and felt she hadn't done all that well on the exams. As it turned out, she was one of the top students in my class and did extremely well. She just didn't like to get freaked out, worried, or upset over something that did absolutely nothing toward her goal. We could do well to follow her lead by keeping our personal performance ... personal.

More than this, our goals should not be to compete with others, but to compete with ourselves. Be the best you can be. Master your study habits to become more efficient and effective. As hard as it might be, forget about everyone else and how they are doing and just do as well as you can.

LAW SCHOOL IS NOT FOREVER

About three months into my first year, after a marathon study session and a particularly hard week of difficult concepts, I felt I had been in law school forever, even though it had only been three months! I found it hard to believe that this kind of abuse would go on for the next two and one-half years. I pushed through, and when I look back on the experience it feels like a dream. Seriously, the entire experience goes by so fast that we often forget to stop and enjoy what we're doing. We all want to do well in life, whether that is being an attorney or a professor or whatever else. Law school is a means to an end, but it should also be something to be enjoyed. After all, you've worked hard to get to this point, and the legal career isn't going to get easier in the foreseeable future—so enjoy the time in law school and remember that it won't last forever. Enjoy it while you can.

PERFORMANCE ON EXAMS

Your performance on exams can go one of three ways: You will have done well and will be pleased, you won't have done so well and will be unhappy, or you'll have hit somewhere in the middle, and will be mostly unhappy. When I use words like well, or not so well, this is all relative to your best performance. If you got a B on an exam, and you know you did everything you could have done and are satisfied with your work, then you did well. On the other hand if you got a B and you know that there was more you could have done, that you could have been a little more effective with your study time, then use it as lesson.

If you're still at the beginning of your time in law school, realize that your first set of exams does not determine your status as a law student, or even how well you will do throughout law school. For those in top law schools who do well, even these first-semester exams are important, as they can determine first-year summer clerkships (because grades will be in just in time for a select few on-campus interviews). Rare but not impossible. For others, good first-semester grades can be helpful in finding jobs in smaller firms, or internships, or part-time positions—all very helpful in helping to pay for law school and in future job prospects. For everyone, these are the first exams you have taken in law school. If you've followed the guidelines in this book, you will have taken your professors' practice exams, but even then, this is the first time you have officially been graded in law school. You should learn from this experience *no matter what grade you receive*. You should analyze which classes you did well in and how your study for that class differed from your study for other classes. Although your exams do label you with a grade, they provide much more information and insight to yourself as a student and how you can do better.

If you did well, good for you. Don't get over-confident though. I saw many of my friends who aced the first round of exams, and then bombed the next round because they became over-confident. If you did well on the first round, you are in a very good place and you of course shouldn't blow it. If anything, you should push a little harder and study a little more so you can outperform yourself on the final exams.

If you hit somewhere in the middle—not great but not bad either, it is time to *step it up*. You got an A or two and a few Bs, and so you are in a good place to look at why you did well in some classes and why you didn't do as well in others. Use the grades to learn and then do better. Apply the best skills and develop the best habits as a law student and aim for better grades in *all* of your classes.

I know several friends who got excellent grades on their first exams who say they wished they had *not* done so well. No joke. They would tell me that because of their great grades from the beginning, they lost steam and became too complacent and lax in their studies. If you didn't do as well on your exams, use this to boost for your performance relative to those who aren't working hard—or working smart. We're all human; we all have bad testing days and you can do better. Remind yourself that you have made it through the rigors of getting *into* law school—and you can use the same energy you used to make it through years of undergraduate school, the LSAT, and intense competition to get the top grades you know are in you.

It's true: Some law students coasted through college simply by being the smartest guy (or gal) in the room. Maybe this includes you. In law school, however, you'll get smacked in the face where *everyone else* is just as smart. It's a real shock to many. Some have poor study habits simply because they never really *studied* before—they never had to. There is no shortage of law students who were anything but the model of studious undergraduates. Now is the time to recognize this issue if it does include you, and prepare to correct this deficiency.

If you bombed your exams, then you really need to re-evaluate your habits. Yes, I know, we've discussed good study habits ad nauseam, but it really comes down to how well (or poorly) you use your time. Only *you* can decide to be better, and the truth is: If you're serious about law school, then you *can* improve your results—by improving your habits. Start by making short, attainable goals and work your way into a strong, sustainable study routine.

Regardless of how you did on the first exam, use it as a motivation builder and keep the attitude positive. Your first semester is only 1/6 of the law school experience (not counting summer clerkships and clinics), and you should take it as such—a jumping off point for the rest of your time in school—and especially for your second semester.

POSITIVE ATTITUDE, ONE MORE TIME

If you really try to enjoy the time you have in school, you will love it. Learning the law won't be quite so hard, and your time won't be quite so stressful. So enjoy it and have fun. You have fun when you make it fun—and all of that is encompassed in having a good attitude. My dad used to say (much to my constant exasperation as a kid) that "your *attitude* determines your *altitude*." I've found that little mantra to be true in many instances—your attitude determines how well you do, how successful you are, and most importantly, how you grow and progress.

8

ACING YOUR FINAL EXAMS

This is where your efforts pay off. Although developing the habits of efficient and effective study will ultimately improve your skills as an attorney, right now you are focused on and concerned about these habits to further one goal: to *ace* your final exams.

This book is a guide to establish basic good habits, at the onset of law school, to make you a more efficient and effective student. If you develop these habits, you will do well and you will be prepared, but even so you still have a fierce beast to face at the end of your courses ... final exams. Law exams are an entity unto themselves, and most students who enter law school have never faced anything quite like it before in their lives. You have three to five hours to answer a few questions. For the most part, your first-year exams will follow this format, so mastery is beneficial. During your second and third years, you will see exams in different formats, which you will likely be more familiar with—multiple choices and take-home exams as well as research papers.

This might not sound perilous, but when you remember that *your entire grade* rests on the shoulders of those few questions, the pressure starts to build. And with every piece of additional information during the year—information that is necessary for the exam—the pressure can get unbearable.

I cannot tell you that the exams aren't hard. They are. But I can tell you that if you are prepared, the experience can actually be pleasant. Instead of a three-hour session of racking your brain or trying to organize your thoughts, you get three hours to show off! It takes work to get to that point, but it is doable. You really can be an efficient and effective student—anyone can do it, and anyone can do it really well. But "doing it" isn't just talking about doing it, or thinking about doing it, but *actually* doing it. Besides the habits necessary to prepare for the exam, it might be a good idea to review an exam-taking routine.

EXAM-TAKING ROUTINE

When you sit down to take your first law exam, you should obviously be prepared with the material you are expected to know. You should also be well prepared for an extended amount of time when you have to think hard and write fast, all the while sitting still among other students who are typing away on their computers. This means that you should have practiced at least one exam for each class. One *full* exam. Most professors will provide past exams with which you can practice—and we've already discussed this as a method of studying *and* preparing. However, these tests can also be beneficial for test-taking practice in itself and developing your own personal strategies. Below are a few pointers to make your practice-exam sessions more beneficial.

Do the things you would do before a regular exam. With your practice exams, you want to create the exam-taking atmosphere as best as you can, so you have a better idea of what it is like.

Time yourself. Part of the stress and strain of a law school exam is the demand to recall a huge amount of information within a set time period. Part of this exercise is being strict about your time. This means that you turn off your cell phone and any and all distractions for the amount of time you are practicing and you focus on the exam. You will be surprised how fast the time goes when you are concentrating so intensely, so it is good to get an idea of how to gauge your progress.

Try and take your practice exams around the same time you will take your real exams. If your exams are going to be in the morning, that it is a good idea to wake up and start your exam whenever your other exams will start, so you get your brain and body used to the idea of sitting and thinking during that time of the day. You probably heard this advice when studying for the LSAT, and it applies here as well. You need your brain to be used to the rigors of exam taking at the time of day when you will take your exams. Otherwise, your brain might not kick into gear until midway through (or even later), which would of course raise some difficulties in the real exam.

Get sample answers from your professors and grade yourself as hard as you can, and then try to do better.

Don't take too many practice exams like this, or you might end up burning out. If you take these practice exams just like you would a real exam, the experience is intense. Just take enough that you are used to sitting down and doing it. No one can tell you when enough is enough—just remember that you've still got to run the marathon. What I did, after taking a few of these practice tests, was practice by outlining the answer to the questions rather than writing them out completely.

YOUR EXAM RITUAL (LEADING UP TO THE ACTUAL EXAM)

If you are prepared, you shouldn't have to cram for the exam the night before. Part of your exam ritual should be going to bed at a decent time the night before. I know I've made a reference to this several times throughout this book, but if you think about your exams the same way you would think about running a marathon, then you will most certainly be prepared. Part of the grueling experience of running a marathon is getting enough sleep before running the race. Likewise, you should get enough sleep before a final exam. You need your brain and body refreshed and awake.

The rest of your ritual can be anything that helps you get your mind going and ready for the exam. I get nervous before tests; so much of my ritual is trying to relax. I stop studying at about 6:00 p.m. the night before the exam, and then focus on having an enjoyable evening. I eat a nice dinner—nothing too heavy—and then I relax with my wife and kids before going to bed at a decent time. I usually do some yoga after waking up, and focus during the pre-exam morning on breathing normally and centering my mind. I have a small breakfast of eggs and toast, and listen to Mozart on the way to school. Brain music! About an hour before the exam, I look over my outline, but nothing too in-depth. By this time, if I don't know it then I certainly won't learn it well enough for the exam. I don't try to "learn" anything at the last minute, and I just try to prepare mentally. You will be in a similar boat, having spent a great deal of time studying and reading and preparing—all of it has passed through your mind and can be recalled.

I want to point out two aspects of my routine that I've already mentioned. The first is a small breakfast of eggs. I read somewhere that eggs have selenium, which is a chemical that affects the brain in positive ways. The article also pointed out that even the smells of cooking eggs is beneficial to getting the brain working fast and that it helps keep your memory sharp. Regardless of the actual effects, I have eaten eggs with the belief that it helps me think better. Maybe eating eggs really does help and maybe it doesn't—maybe all I've done is give myself some version of a placebo and I only believe that it is helping me think more clearly. Whatever eggs do, however, I am convinced that I perform better when I eat a nice egg breakfast.

Likewise, I've read studies that say if you listen to Mozart you are able to recall information more easily. I've read other studies that say this just isn't so, and if it is, then the improvement is minimal. Whatever the actual effect, I've convinced myself that I can remember things faster and more clearly when I listen to Mozart prior to taking exams. It is an added assurance that I am doing everything in my power to do well—including stimulating my mind and getting it ready for the exam.

I strongly believe that you should use these positive assurances in putting your brain in proper working order. It is the whole idea behind the pre-exam ritual. You do things because it makes you feel better, it decreases anxiety, and it helps you think more clearly. The whole point of the semester prior to the final exam is to prepare for the final exam, and I view the moments just before the exam as a time to clear the mind and focus my thoughts and energies on doing well. However you focus on doing well is up to you, but it is important to do something.

How Professors Write Exams

Professors write exams to contain as many legal issues as possible. You will be surprised to find out just how much can go into an exam question. Most exam questions are like a story—or a fact pattern—that tells of some interaction or event happening that you, as a lawyer, need to evaluate. At first, it might not seem like there is much going on in the question, but as you dig deeper, you will realize that loads of legal questions and issues can be packed tightly into exams. You should keep this in mind: that no matter how many issues you have found, there are probably more in there.

Law exams are set up to test your knowledge of the course and are constructed to capture the *forest* rather than the trees, mostly. Remember earlier as we discussed outlining and studying: that you should focus on the forest rather than the trees. Here is where this type of thinking pays off. Each exam will have many, many trees—or facts—but the focus is how those details work together as a whole—the forest. Therefore, you should focus on the big issues and work your way to the smaller issues (and smaller and smaller issues still, if you have time), as it is the bigger issues that will get you more points on the exam.

Consider this example, using the forest and the trees analogy. Let's say that a professor sits you down with a large picture of rolling hills blanketed with trees. For purely aesthetic purposes, let's say that it is autumn and the leaves are brilliantly colored. The professor asks you to describe the forest and tells you that you will be graded based on your description. So you go about analyzing the shadows from one clump of trees and how the shadow affects another group of trees. You look at dips in the rolling hills, and high points, how the sun is reflected. Several of the individual trees are prominent, and you briefly pay attention to those, but your main focus is on the forest as a whole and how all the trees work together to create the picturesque scene before you. The professor returns and you find that you missed a few things, but for the most part you did what was asked. The professor asked you to describe the forest, not particular branches or leaves or twigs or silkworms. Had you focused your attention on each individual branch or leaf, you could never have seen how the trees work together, because there is simply not enough time to get every leaf and every branch into your description without leaving out another, equally important leaf or branch.

This is how the law school exam works: Your professor can't possibly hit every detail, because there are too many details and caveats in the law, and if you highlight one, then others are just as important and probably should be mentioned. It's a slippery slope of information. Sure, a few of the prominent details will be there—but for the most part you are writing about how all the legal concepts you've studied work together to create "Contract Law" or "Constitutional Law."

Now does it also make sense why you must get comfortable writing quickly? There is simply no time for lazy writing habits in law school. The law exam is *very* fast-paced, and there are nearly always a few extra details that might be added in that last minute of the exam.

So, while the details are interesting and good to know, they should not be the *focus* of your studies, or in your answers to the final exams. Not only will you miss the big picture, but you could end up spending all of your time on the details of one question and not nearly enough time on the main points of any other question. It's also likely that you'll miss a big issue entirely, resulting in many lost points.

How Professors Grade Exams

The ideas above lead to another habit of professors, which is to divide up the points and sometimes the time allotted for each question. For example, say that there are 3 questions on the exam. You would think that each question is worth the same amount of points. But often, this assumption is wrong. Usually a professor will have a "main" question, which will count for more points than the other questions and will contain a mountain of legal issues. The professor will then throw in a few more questions that are worth less, but analyze smaller issues, or policy concerns within that area of law, or even in some pet area of the professor's interest. All of these questions are important, of course, but more attention should obviously be given to the question that is worth more points.

Each question will have a set of issues, and an accompanying set of rules, legal concepts, and case law that the professor expects you to explain and cite. Her grading sheet will probably look similar to your outline, giving more points for the bigger issues, and fewer points to smaller issues. For example, you might get 5 points each for mention cases A and B and rule Z, while only getting 1 point for discussing the dissent in the opinion for case A. Please see the sample grading sheet, below, for fuller details of how this works.

CRAMMING FOR EXAMS

No. If you are prepared, you shouldn't have to cram for the exam. If you have to cram, you're already behind the legal 8-ball. *If* you find yourself in need of cramming, here are a few pointers:

Start cramming as early in the day as possible. Yes, for many the idea of cramming is to go late into the night, pushing absolutely as much information into your brain as possible. However, remember that you will have to write comprehendible sentences the next day, and being tired does not work. So start cramming as *early* as possible so you can go to bed early enough to get a good night's sleep. In many ways, the sleep might be more important to your exam performance than the cramming.

Avoid caffeine and other stimulants. Instead, eat energizing foods that provide the same amount of stimuli—just in a form that your body will better use. If you don't already have an idea of these types of foods, research this before you're in law school, such as by typing "Healthy Food for Energy" in Google. If your body is already used to stimulants like caffeine, then it probably isn't a good idea to stop caffeine intake immediately before an exam. Remember, avoid sudden lifestyle changes in law school! The idea is not to put anything into your body that it isn't already used to. That said, I will re-emphasize that you want to be healthy and not consume stimulants that make you *feel* more energized, but then later send you crashing.

Cram for only short periods of a time, taking short breaks. Don't overdo it only to burn out. If you have to, set an alarm so you only study for 20 minutes at a time, and then take a five-minute break.

Don't rewrite you notes, or spend time formatting outlines, or even re-digesting all of your notes. If you've followed the steps in this book, you will find your study sessions much better, as you will have already prepared outlines and have already spent time going over this material. There won't be "cramming" because there won't be a need to cram. If worse comes to worse, read over your class notes and briefs *once*—to derive quickly as much of the professor's nuances as you can, and then focus on the black letter law found in commercial outlines. Even though your professor might have deviated from how commercial outlines are structured, the law is the same and you can get the main points and concepts from reading the black letter law. Study from commercial outlines, past exams, outlines from students who have already taken the class, anything you can get your hands on.

Again, *you do not want to cram!* Be *prepared* for your exams instead.

YET MORE ADDITIONAL TIPS ON EXAMS

Maintain control over your breathing throughout the exam. Focus on breathing as you read and write. Practice this.

Realize that the mental strain is half the challenge. The exams are meant to put you on the spot and make you think hard. Breathing helps in reducing strain and in getting oxygen to your brain.

Read the exam instructions—every line—so as to not miss anything the professor expects.

Read the entire exam first so you know what you are getting yourself into. This relates to the section on how professors divided the questions and how they grade the exams. One time I answered the second question within the first question without realizing it, because I never read beyond the first question. I ended up wasting a *lot* of time.

Outline your question before writing down any of the answer. Get the big concepts and then work yourself through the elements.

Look at each element from every angle you can. Remember, if something is understood to be slightly different, the entire answer could change. Explore all possible angles and perspectives.

Be fast, but be organized. Use clear, short sentences. I have a friend who would have done extremely well on an exam had she been better organized.

Stick to the allotted time frame for each question.

For *every* issue, state the issue, your rationale, your analysis, and your conclusion. Most professors don't care much what your conclusion is (unless it's way off base); they want to see you work through the issue and analyze all the possibilities. So, everything *before* the conclusion is key.

You don't need to use clever transitions from one part of a question to another. Use subheadings.

Don't repeat the facts—start with the legal issues. You are showing the professor that you have learned the law and can analyze the issues based on the facts.

Once you are finished, relax and spend a few hours decompressing. Then get cracking on your next exam.

9

Sample Exam And Answer Key

The law school exam can be elusive, in that it's hard to know what to expect. When one doesn't know what to expect, it is likewise hard to know what to study and how to study to take your exam most effectively. Below you will find a sample exam question, written by a real, live law professor. You will also find a sample answer and the grading key for the question! This law professor was, in fact, one of my 1L professors, and the question you see is the same question I faced when I was in your shoes.

I include these materials for several reasons, the first of which is to give you a sense of the "flavor" of law exams. As you can usually get a sample exam from your professor, this is key to get a taste for what *your* exam is likely to be like. The benefit of showing you *this* exam is that you can read a real exam and see how the development of the habits in this book will lead to your success. You will see why it's important to read effectively, why you condensed your outlines, and why you followed the other advice and suggested habits in this book. It's all geared toward this singular goal.

So take a look! You might not understand the many issues in the exam and in the sample answer—don't worry, you soon will—but that's not the point here: Pay attention to the way the question is constructed, and how the answers to these types of questions are constructed. Most importantly, study the grading sheet. This is how many professors grade, and any insight on how to get more points is invaluable.

SAMPLE EXAM

CONTRACTS (PROFESSOR SETTY)

FACT PATTERN

Stephanie owns MyStyles Boutique, a retailer of women's clothing. In May 2009, Stephanie enters into a contract with Farouk, who designs and manufactures handmade sweaters, to purchase 50 sweaters from him. The contract states that Stephanie "will display, promote, and sell Farouk's designs from August 1 through October 15, 2009." Stephanie bought the sweaters for $50 each, and plans to sell them at $70 each. Under the agreement, Farouk would receive an additional $5 per sweater that Stephanie sells.

In August 2009, Stephanie enters into negotiations with Wanda, a designer and manufacturer of women's winter coats from whom Stephanie has bought coats each of the past three years. Each of the past three years, she's sold about 20 of Wanda's coats. During the August 2009 negotiations at Wanda's office, it becomes clear to Stephanie that Wanda has a larger than usual inventory of coats. Stephanie wonders to herself whether the large inventory is there because Wanda hasn't secured deals with other retailers. Instead of ordering 20 coats from Wanda this year, Stephanie proposes that she purchase five coats from Wanda up front for $100 per coat, and additional coats at the same price from Wanda on an "as needed" basis through November 1, 2009. Wanda agrees to this arrangement, and agrees to deliver the five coats on October 1.

Stephanie leaves the meeting with Wanda, but as she waits for the elevator in Wanda's office, Stephanie overhears two of Wanda's employees talking about how George, the owner of Gotta Have It, a rival boutique to MyStyles, is thinking about ordering 50 of Wanda's winter coats this year.

Stephanie, now worried, emails Wanda that afternoon with the following message: "Following up on our deal, I wanted to make sure that you will forbear from selling coats to anybody else before letting me know first." Wanda replies 30 seconds later: "Sure."

On October 1, 2009, at the MyStyles boutique, Farouk's sweaters are displayed prominently at the front of the store, as they have been since August 1. In August, Stephanie sold 25 of Farouk's sweaters. From September 1-15, she sold 8 of his sweaters. From September 16-30, she sold 7 of Farouk's sweaters.

Stephanie removes Farouk's 10 remaining sweaters from the front of the store, and re-stocks them in a back corner behind the "Clearance" rack, still priced at $70 per sweater.

She unpacks the box of Wanda's winter coats that arrived that morning, and displays them in the front of MyStyles, priced at $200 each. She sells all five coats that afternoon and has to turn away three more customers looking for Wanda's coats. Stephanie phones Wanda, and tries to order an additional 25 coats. Wanda tells her that she doesn't have any more coats to sell, as she sold her remaining inventory to George in mid-September.

Between October 1 and October 15, no additional sweaters of Farouk's have been sold. Customers repeatedly ask for Wanda's coats at MyStyles, and Stephanie turns them away. Over at Gotta Have It, George priced Wanda's coats at $300 each, and sold 25 of them.

ESSAY (IN YOUR ANSWER, ADDRESS ALL SUBPARTS):

Describe and analyze the strength of the potential contract claims (if any) of the following individuals.

Stephanie
Farouk

ANSWER TO SAMPLE EXAM, PROF. SETTY

ESSAY

Part (a): Stephanie's potential contract claims

Stephanie has potential breach of contract claims against Wanda on numerous grounds:

First, the agreement between Stephanie and Wanda qualifies as a requirements contract, and, as such, is a valid contract with consideration (and not an illusory promise under R2K 77). Following the rationale of the court in the Eastern Air Lines case, requirements contracts are bilateral contracts in which the promise of Wanda to provide Stephanie with as many coats "as needed" constitutes consideration. Under Eastern, Wanda is obligated to make a good faith effort to provide Stephanie with the usual number of coats that Stephanie normally purchased from her, allowing for some flexibility between the parties for changes in supply and demand.

Wanda could (and should) argue that the contract was illusory under R2K 77, and attempt to distinguish it from <u>Eastern</u> by saying that in <u>Eastern</u>, the parties had specifically negotiated and entered into a requirements contract numerous times, and that was the standard arrangement between them. In the current situation, Stephanie's usual practice was to purchase 20 coats per year outright, but she chose not to do that this year. By doing so, Stephanie gave up the right to require a certain number of coats, and Wanda had the right to sell them to any other customer, since there was no advance indication from Stephanie that she would need additional coats.

In response to this claim, Stephanie should argue that the terms of the contract were as follows: Stephanie pays $500; in exchange, she receives from Wanda five coats plus the right to purchase more coats "as needed." This is far more than a peppercorn of consideration for the right to purchase additional coats.

Although there are significant differences in the given fact pattern and the facts in <u>Eastern</u>, a court would likely ultimately side with Stephanie that a valid requirements contract existed and was breached by Wanda's lack of good faith effort in providing Stephanie with the coats.

<u>Second</u>, Stephanie could attempt to allege breach of contract based on the email exchange after the negotiations between Stephanie and Wanda, but this would likely be unsuccessful. Although forbearance is a valid form of consideration (<u>see Hamer, Fiege</u>), in the fact pattern there was no bargained-for exchange for Wanda's forbearance. Stephanie offered nothing more to Wanda as consideration, and therefore the email exchange was not supported by consideration under R2K 71 and 75. Like the situations in <u>Strong v. Sheffield</u>, and to a lesser extent in <u>Mills v. Wyman, Kirksey, and Feinberg</u>, although one party may have believed that an enforceable promise was being made, there was no consideration for that promise. (<u>See also R2K 77</u>).

<u>Third</u>, Stephanie could try to plead reliance to enforce Wanda's email promise to forbear from selling coats to anybody else without prior notice to Stephanie, but this would likely fail. Under <u>D&G Stout</u> and R2K 90, and to a lesser extent under <u>Ricketts, Feinberg, and Cohen</u>, Stephanie would need to show that Wanda made a promise, that Wanda made the promise with the understanding (from an objective perspective) that Stephanie would rely on the promise, that Stephanie actually did rely on the promise, and that a grave injustice was being suffered by Stephanie in order for a court to make a promise unsupported by consideration enforceable. According to the facts given here, although

Wanda's "sure" could possibly be considered a promise, there is no indication that Wanda made her comment with the intention that Stephanie would rely on it. Further, there is no indication that Stephanie suffered to such an extent that a court would feel obligated to invoke reliance.

Fourth, Stephanie could attempt to make a restitution claim against Wanda for the coats, stating that even though there was no enforceable promise by Wanda to forbear from selling her coats elsewhere, Wanda was unjustly enriched by selling the coats to George. The fact pattern here does not support such a finding, since there is no indication that Stephanie conferred a benefit on Wanda, who was then unjustly enriched by the sale of coats to George (see Callano, R2K 370, 371). A restitution claim would almost definitely fail.

Fifth, Stephanie could try to argue that the email exchange constituted an exclusive arrangement and that Wanda, under the rationale of Lucy, Lady Duff-Gordon, was obligated to act in good faith to fulfill it. This would be a losing argument, since even the email exchange, on its face, doesn't establish an exclusive relationship between the parties.

Sixth, as an aside, even if Wanda is obligated to satisfy Stephanie's order under the requirements contract, it may make more sense for her to efficiently breach that contract if the deal with George ends up being more lucrative for her. She would then have to pay expectation damages to Stephanie based on that breach.

Part (b): Farouk's potential contract claims

Farouk has a potential breach of contract claim against Stephanie under their agreement to "display, promote and sell" his sweaters through October 15. Stephanie upheld her end of the contract through October 1, but for the last two weeks, she shifted his sweaters to an inconspicuous corner of the store, at which point none of them sold. Under the rationale of USNI, Stephanie's action qualifies as a breach of the agreement between her and Farouk since she was not acting in good faith by moving the sweaters, and he should seek and receive his expectation damages as compensation (see R2K 347).

Stephanie should argue that she did not breach the contract, since the sweaters were still for sale within the store and were technically still "displayed," and arguably "promoted." She could try to argue that the sales in Farouk's sweaters were declining anyway, and there's no indication that any of his sweaters would have sold between October 1 and 15 had they been in the front of the store. Based on the facts here, this argument would likely fail, and Farouk's argument would prevail.

Here, it seems that Stephanie efficiently breached the contract with Farouk by putting aside items that weren't selling well and promoting Wanda's coats instead, which were good sellers.

SAMPLE EXAM: SCORING SHEET

ESSAY, PART (A), STEPHANIE'S CLAIMS: 47 POSSIBLE POINTS

Stephanie's argument re: "as needed" contract:

Discussion Point	Possible Points	Points Awarded
Consideration for "as needed" contract under R2K 71	3	
Requirements contract	3	
Analysis under Eastern Air Lines	3	
Illusory under R2K 77?	2	
Wanda obligated to make a good faith effort	3	
Parties allowed some flexibility re: supply & demand	2	
Entire contract was: $500 in exchange for 5 coats plus "as needed" availability (peppercorn)	2	
Reliance/Promissory Estoppel Theory:		
Discussion of Reliance/Promissory Estoppel	2	
Analysis under R2K 90 (consider whether factors are listed)	3	
Analysis under case law: D&G Stout, Ricketts, Feinberg, Cohen	3	
Subtotal		

Wanda's rebuttal argument re: "as needed" contract:

Discussion Point	Possible Points	Points Awarded
Discussion of illusory contract under R2K 77	2	
Distinguishable from <u>Eastern</u> on history between parties?	1	
No indication that Stephanie would want additional coats, since Stephanie is the one initiating the change in the agreement from previous years	1	
Efficient breach based on expected profit from George	2	
Subtotal		

Re: email exchange:

Discussion Point	Possible Points	Points Awarded
Forbearance can be a valid form of consideration	2	
Analysis under <u>Hamer, Fiege</u>	2	
Is there bargained-for exchange here?	2	
Analysis under R2K 71, 75	3	
Analysis under <u>Strong v. Sheffield, Mattel v. Hopper</u>	2	
Analysis under other authority: <u>Mills, Feinberg, Kirksey</u>, R2K 77	2	
Subtotal		

Other possible arguments:

Discussion Point	Possible Points	Points Awarded
Restitution Theory: —unlikely to be a winning argument, since no benefit conferred, no unjust enrichment (citation to <u>Callano</u>, R2K 370, 371)	1	
Exclusivity Arrangement: —unlikely to be a winning argument, since no exclusivity demanded by the email reference (analysis under <u>Wood</u>)	1	
Subtotal		
Notes or Questions from Grader:		

ESSAY, PART (B), FAROUK'S CLAIMS: 19 POSSIBLE POINTS

Farouk's claim:

Discussion Point	Possible Points	Points Awarded
Breach of contract based on moving display early, not being promoted after the move to the back of the store	3	
Evidenced by lack of sales in new location compared to old location	2	
Analysis under <u>USNI</u> (Naval Institute v. Berkeley)	3	
Analysis of good faith effort by Stephanie	1	
What type of damages should be sought? (likely expectation)	2	
Cite to R2K 347, 344, 349	2	
Subtotal		

Stephanie's rebuttal:

Discussion Point	Possible Points	Points Awarded
No breach because sweaters were still in the store and for sale (technically still displayed)	2	
Even if there's a breach, there should be no or nominal damages, since it's unlikely that Farouk's sweaters would have sold anyway	1	
Efficient breach based on higher profit margin with Wanda's coats	3	
Subtotal		

THE GRADING SHEET

Pay particular attention to the grading sheet. Although there are multiple issues for each answer, the list of issues does not go on without end. This is not magic!

You must focus on the big issues *and* work your way to smaller details, but you cannot spend too much time on details—not in your reading and study, nor in your exam answer. One of the main keys to being an effective student is doing only what you need to do, and doing it very, very well. If you have time, learn the nuances, sure—but don't obsess about those smaller issues on the exam. Usually, you'll be fighting just to get all of the main issues into your answer before the time is up. Get all the main answers right, and you get an "A"!

Law school exams are difficult—but doable. If you are prepared, if you implement the good habits discussed in this book, you will do all right.

10

Good Habits, Good Start

So that's it! A few essential habits that will help you attain your goals as a law student. The idea is to start attaining these habits as soon as possible, prior to and during your very first week of law school.

If you're reading this little book after your first week—or anytime in law school for that matter—remember that it's never too late to improve. The idea is to be effective and to use your time as a student as efficiently as possible.

If you follow the advice and tips in this book, not only will you do well on your exams, but you'll also have a more enjoyable law school experience. You'll have more time to keep being you, to do the things you love, to have fun—all the while being a successful law student who does well on exams and who is the presence in class everyone wants to befriend.

Best of luck to you!

About the Author

Derrick Hibbard placed in the top 15% of his first-year class and as a dean's honor student at the University of Miami School of Law. Among other law school accomplishments, the author received the CALI Award for highest grade in Property Law.

Besides a legal career, Derrick is a horror aficionado—as to film, books, and law school. He is also an amateur filmmaker, screenwriter, and novelist. Along with this, his first book, Hibbard has written and published a Christmas play as well as stories and articles in various journals.

When not in the world of law, Derrick has worked with Habitat for Humanity and spent time working in an orphanage and school in Lusaka, Zambia.

INDEX

S

T

U

V-Z

OTHER BOOKS

GRAINS OF GOLDEN SAND: ADVENTURES IN WAR-TORN AFRICA,
by Delfi Messinger
Hardcover 978-1-888960-35-8,
391 pages, US$21.95
Softcover 1-888960-33-4,
391 pages, US$15.95

Grab a ticket for the adventure of a
lifetime: meet a woman who protects
rare apes by painting, in blood, SIDA
("AIDS" in French) on a Kinshasa
wall to keep rampaging looters at bay.

Her mission was to save a small group of endangered great apes—the
bonobo (or "sexy" ape)—from the grip of civil war in the heart of Zaire.
She made this her mission, and after eight harrowing years the reader
will be breathless with amazement in her struggles to get the endangered animals to safety.

TRAINING WHEELS FOR STUDENT LEADERS: A JUNIOR COUNSELING
PROGRAM IN ACTION, by Autumn Messinger
ISBN 978-1-888960-13-6, US$21.95

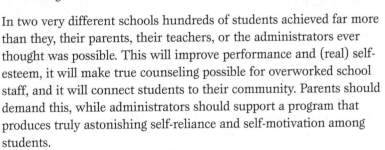

A reference for the engaged parent,
founded on the premise that, if given the
opportunity, mentoring, and guidance,
even young children can work together
to solve (and resolve) their own
problems. They can work towards their
own, common, cooperative goals. They
can build genuine self-esteem.

In two very different schools hundreds of students achieved far more
than they, their parents, their teachers, or the administrators ever
thought was possible. This will improve performance and (real) self-
esteem, it will make true counseling possible for overworked school
staff, and it will connect students to their community. Parents should
demand this, while administrators should support a program that
produces truly astonishing self-reliance and self-motivation among
students.

The Art Of The Law School Transfer: A Guide to Gransferring Law Schools, By Andrew B. Carrabis and Seth D. Haimovitch
ISBN 978-1-888960-30-3, 160 pg, US$16.95

Transferring from one law school to another is like painting a panorama. There are the technical elements, sure. Failing to follow these can make colors sag and smear, destroying all that's done to that point. In law school, that's a lifetime of academic preparation. As with all works of art, there's an artistic element as well. It's not enough to simply submit papers and files on time. The transfer process is full of quirks that a novice—any novice—will not see coming. With this book new students will be prepared, and will prepare their own works of art. After years of effort and sacrifice, don't ruin a portrait with needless errors. Instead, create the masterpiece that will get you into the law school of your dreams.

Later-in-Life Lawyers: Tips for the Non-Traditional Law Student, by Charles Cooper
ISBN 978-1-888960-06-8, 288 pg, US$18.95

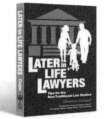

Law school is a scary place for any new student. For an older ("non-traditional") student, it can be intimidating as well as ill-designed for the needs of a student with children, mortgages, and the like. Includes advice on families and children; the LSAT, GPAs, application process, and law school rankings for non-traditional students; paying for law school; surviving first year; non-academic hurdles; and the occasional skeleton in the non-traditional closet. This book is a must-read for the law student who is not going directly from college to law school.

The Slacker's Guide to Law School: Success Without Stress, by Juan Doria
ISBN 978-1-888960-52-5, 162 pg, US$16.95

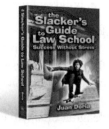

It is easy to fall into a trap of assuming that one either strives and succeeds or slacks and fails. Enjoying three years of law school is not the opposite of learning the law. There's also a tendency to follow a herd mentality: the assumption that there's just one right way to do something, or just one way to study the law. Too often, this involves too much make-work and too much stress. This book will show you how to do law school right: success without stress. (Or at least with *less* stress.)

FOR THE LAW STUDENT

LAW SCHOOL: GETTING IN, GETTING GOOD, GETTING THE GOLD,
by Thane Messinger
ISBN: 978-1-888960-80-8, 367 pages, US$16.95

The key in successful law study is a minimum
of wasted effort and a maximum of results. Still
outlining cases? A waste of time. Failing to use
hypotheticals? A dangerous omission.
Preparing a huge outline? A dangerous waste
of time. Don't waste your time, and don't
neglect what's truly important. Learn law school techniques that work.
Once you're in, Get Good, and Get the Gold!

THE INSIDER'S GUIDE TO GETTING A BIG FIRM JOB: WHAT EVERY LAW
STUDENT SHOULD KNOW ABOUT INTERVIEWING,
by Erika M Finn and Jessica T. Olmon
ISBN-13 978-1-888960-14-3, 130 pages,
US$16.95

The competition for top jobs is intense, and the
special needs of law firm recruiters are
unknown to most law students. Most books
aimed at law students speak to how to get into
law school, and how to succeed in law school, but none address how to
get a lucrative job. This book is an insider's look at the secrets of landing a dream law firm job.

PLANET LAW SCHOOL II: WHAT YOU NEED TO KNOW (BEFORE YOU GO)—
BUT DIDN'T KNOW TO ASK ... AND NO ONE ELSE WILL TELL YOU,
by Atticus Falcon
ISBN 978-1-888960-50-7, 858 pages, US$24.95

An encyclopedic reference. Examines hundreds
of sources, and offers in-depth advice on law
courses, materials, methods, study guides, professors, attitude, examsmanship, law review,
internships, research assistantships, clubs, clinics, law jobs, dual degrees, advanced law
degrees, MBE, MPRE, bar review options, and the bar exam. Sets out all
that a law student must master to excel in law school.

For the New Attorney

JAGGED ROCKS OF WISDOM: PROFESSIONAL ADVICE FOR THE NEW
ATTORNEY, by Morten Lund
ISBN: 978-1-888960-07-5, US$18.95

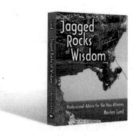

Written by a top partner, this no-nonsense
guide is a must-have for the new associate. Its
"21 Rules of Law Office Life" will help make
the difference to your success in the law: surviving your first years as an attorney, and
making partner. Beware. Avoid the dangers.
Read, read, and read again these 21 Rules of
Law Office Life.

JAGGED ROCKS OF WISDOM—THE MEMO: MASTERING THE LEGAL
MEMORANDUM, by Morten Lund
ISBN: 978-1-888960-08-6, US$18.95
This book focuses on one of the most complex

aspects of professional work for a new attorney: researching, drafting, and refining the
legal memorandum. This book breaks the
process of the legal memorandum into "21
Rules." In these rules the mysteries are
revealed. The process and survival will be no
less arduous, but with this book the journey
will not be as treacherous.

THE YOUNG LAWYER'S JUNGLE BOOK: A SURVIVAL GUIDE,
by Thane Messinger
ISBN 978-1-888960-19-1, US$18.95
A career guide for summer associates,
judicial clerks, and all new attorneys. Now in
its 14th year and second edition, hundreds of

sections with advice on law office life, advice
on law office life, including working with
senior attorneys, legal research and writing,
memos, contract drafting, mistakes, grammar,
email, managing workload, timesheets, annual
reviews, teamwork, department, attitude, perspective, working with
clients (and dissatisfied clients), working with office staff, using office
tools, and yes, much more.

Recommended in the ABA's *Law Practice Management* and *The
Compleat Lawyer,* as well as in numerous state bar journals.